The Allotment
new lyric poets

– Stride –

Also available from Stride:

Binary Myths 1 & 2 edited by Andy Brown

Hunting the Kinnayas Andy Brown

Nekyia Rose Flint

The Solex Brothers Luke Kennard

The Lady Chapel Sarah Law

Bliss Tangle Sarah Law

The Glaze from Breaking Joanne Merriam

The Allotment
new lyric poets

edited by
Andy Brown

THE ALLOTMENT
First edition 2006
© 2006
All rights reserved

Selection and Introduction © Andy Brown

Copyright of individual contributions
remains with individual contributors

ISBN 1-905024-07-X

Cover design by Neil Annat
Cover painting: 'Wessex Landscape' 1982
© Brian Rice 1982, 2006
Used by kind permission of the artist

Published by
Stride Publications
11 Sylvan Road, Exeter
Devon EX4 6EW
England

www.stridebooks.co.uk

Contents

Introduction

allotment / *n*. **1** a small piece of land rented for cultivation. **2** garden plot, kitchen garden, patch, tract, plot. **3** a share allotted **4** ration, quota, lot, measure

1. New...?

In their various ways, the poets gathered in this anthology each demonstrate innovative handlings of the Lyric. My selection of writers is partisan and non-exhaustive: this is not a complete summary of contemporary lyric poets, nor could an anthology of this size ever pretend to be so. Instead, here is a personal selection of relatively new writers who range from Britain, to Canada, India, Europe and the Middle East. They similarly range from those who have already published notable early collections and several who have won Eric Gregory Awards in recent years, to those who are just beginning to publish their work. Each of them, I believe, successfully achieves a synthesis and tension between two key elements in lyric poetry: newness and tradition.

The interplay of these elements in twentieth century poetics has been well documented and, if one is not already familiar with the developments, T.S. Eliot's 'Tradition and the Individual Talent' (1919), Charles Olson's 'Projective Verse' (1950), Helen Vendler's *Soul Says* (1995), or the writings of Seamus Heaney in *Finders Keepers: selected prose 1971-2001*, to name but four eclectic waymarkers in a century of vociferous debate, should offer varied and enlightening perspectives.[1] It is not my intention to rehearse the critical arguments here, for this is an anthology of poetry and the poems must speak for themselves. But a few contextual words on the rationale of my selection might I hope be of use.

In attempting to represent some innovations with the Lyric, I have not restricted myself to the narrow tradition that is sometimes referred to as 'linguistically innovative' poetry, although certain of the poets here might seem to belong to that tradition. What I am interested in trying to represent, however, are wider issues of formal, imaginative and intellectual innovation – the *How?* the *Why?* and the *What?* of a lyric poem – in a range of poets from a range of writing traditions. Literary innovation has never been, I believe, something that solely takes place *outside of* the mainstream, for a number of reasons. Firstly, innovation is not simply a matter of advanced, or avant-garde technique. Rather, innovation depends upon a tension struck between tradition and newness – between *what comes before* and *what we expect* to come next. I mean this, not only in terms of the development of traditions across time, but also within individual's books, and within the individual poem, where linear syntax or vertical parataxis play with reader expectations. Innovation exists in the gaps between expectations and desires. New meanings are generated in the tension between intention and contingency but, since it is obviously an intentional poet who makes the poem, the situation must be a matter of some intentional control; or a recognition at least that the reader also has a key role to play in the generation of meanings that a poem may hint at. I therefore most often find innovation within the tension between control ('technique' and 'craft'), and lack of control (language as a resistant medium). Innovation resides where imagination and reality rub shoulders or – to return to the Modernist Lyric of Wallace Stevens – the representation of disorder within order: 'Oh! Blessed rage for order, pale Ramon'[2]. In exploring these tensions, innovative lyric poetries lend their strategies and techniques a vigorous work-out along the edge of predictability; they investigate the possibilities of yielding up to, or disrupting, expectations and desires; something the poets in this anthology are all notably aware of.

A second reason I distrust the notional polarity of 'innovation' and 'tradition', is that the opposition, like many binary oppositions, is based upon false premises. The notion that all noteworthy progression and development in writing is handled by an elite avant-garde of writers whose fingers alone are on the zeitgeist buttons of innovation, I find unhelpful. Instead, I have always felt that if one actually looks to *the side of* where people say 'it's at' in terms of 'the cutting edge', well, that's usually where, in fact, it *is* at. Which provides me with my first disclaimer: I am not arguing that this anthology is 'where it's at, and here alone', although I do believe these writers are certainly strongly present in the right locale. In a recent article in *Strong Words*, Anne Stevenson offers salutary words on this matter, decrying mainstream and avant garde fashions in poetry, to identify her ideal poem of the twenty-first century as one to be written by 'a poet who is in thrall to nothing but poetry's weird tyranny and ungovernable need to exist'.[3]

That is how I feel about the poets gathered here – these are neither writers brought together beneath the banner of a manifesto, nor in the formation of a School. They find themselves together because each writes poems that have that 'ungovernable need to exist'; a need I cherish in all writing, whatever its persuasions and traditions.

A third reason I distrust the polarities of 'newness' and 'tradition' (a polarity that does much disservice to poetry through the maintenance of 'Them vs. Us', 'Mainstream vs. Innovative' boundaries) lies in the un-arguable plurality of poetry in recent decades. Given this plurality, even the existence of a recognisable and unified avant-garde seems questionable. Rather than a progressive avant-garde, we seem to now have something that more approximates a *rhizomatic*[4] body-poetic; one that sends out runners in many different directions, testing boundaries and developing strategies when changes in approach are required. When one considers that many of the techniques employed by linguistically innovative poets are techniques that have been used for a very long time – collage, assemblage, cut-up, found poems, concretion, mathematical formulas etc., – it becomes nonsensical to think of these any longer as 'innovations'. They are an embedded part of literary practice and are exploited by writers across the creative spectra. It was 1920 when T.S. Eliot wrote

> Immature poets imitate; mature poets steal; bad poets deface what they take, and good poets make it into something better, or at least something different.[5]

The plundering that Eliot proposed – and which was, perhaps, practised to the point of exhaustion by the Dadaists and Futurists in the early years of the twentieth century – survived well through the radical changes of Modernism, Postmodernism and into the present day, even as the tortured magician of postmodernism fades away, revealing the secrets of its self-referential tricks as it does so.[6] Not that the actual naming or claiming of 'innovation' actually matters beyond the demands of defining, or marketing poets as part of a particular School or camp. Such so-called 'Modernist techniques' as collage, assemblage, or the recycling of existing materials in Kurt Schwitters' *Merz*[7] for example, might even be argued to find their antecedents in the Byzantine *Centos* (Christian texts composed of passages from the epics of the Greeks). As exemplar of his own dictum, Eliot famously admitted lines from Goldsmith, Baudelaire and Verlaine, to name but a few; Pound used a copious fragment of the *Odyssey* to open one of his *Cantos* and Jorge Louis Borges' mythical writer Cesar Paladion annexed the complete opus of Herera, granting Herera's book his own name… 'neither admitting or omitting a single comma'. So what exactly is the smallest, or largest, unit a writer can use without accusations of plagiarism, or mere ventriloquism; and how can a writer at the start of the twenty-first century using these same techniques claim to be 'innovative' simply on the basis of techniques? Where in the continuum does the innovation actually reside?

Most technologies evolve by hybridising, by developing older tools and materials; not an outright rejection of those that came before. Language, as a technology – and poetry as an imaginative embodiment of that technology – is no different. Innovation implies precursors; simple binary oppositions about 'breaking with the past', or operating 'outside of mainstream literary tradition' are simply unhelpful and, at worst, damaging. Unhelpful, because divisive and used as a tool for maintaining antagonisms between writers themselves. Damaging, because reductive; defining the imaginative faculties and processes of poetry as tools for opposition only. Within the context of my 'allotment' then, the innovative Lyric might be seen as 'a small plot of land rented from plural traditions for cultivation'.

2. *Lyric…?*

Which brings me to the choice of defining this anthology as one of new Lyric poets. Lyric is one of poetry's ancient categories, alongside those of Narrative or Epic, and Dramatic poetry. Again, discourse and descriptions of the Lyric are manifold and it is not my intention to rehearse them here, although I would like to foreground the *music* of the Lyric as primarily attractive to me as a reader of these individual voices.[8] But Lyric is neither simply written with musical structures in mind, nor simply with the non-linguistic ('felt' or 'emotional') elements of music in mind. Such a definition might lead to confused 'methods of dealing with the paradoxical nature of a "musical" poetry which [is] no longer literally "melodic".'[9] I am mindful here of Basil Bunting's extensive commentary on the matter of music and poetry, most notably

> Poetry, like music is to be heard... Prose exists to convey meaning, and no meaning such as prose conveys can be expressed as well in poetry. That is not poetry's business. Poetry is seeking to make not meaning, but beauty; or if you insist on misusing words, its 'meaning' is of another kind, and lies in the relation of one another of lines and patterns of sound... which the hearer feels rather than understands.[10]

Bunting's insistence on 'feeling' here is paramount. Given the plurality of late 20th and early 21st Century voices – both in society in general and, specifically, the poetry that reflects those societies – self-expression *per se* has been superseded by a wide range of social and political critiques, all deeply felt. As such it is not difficult to understand the continuing relevance of the Lyric both to poetic and social discourse. With deconstructionist critics 'finding unconvincing and inadequate the critical postulation that the speaker of the Lyric was the poet himself, or even a fictive persona',[11] contemporary lyric poetry has exploded in an unprecedented volume of 'voiced' poems,[12] so that 'the speaker [has become] a device for making the invisible visible'.[13] To return to my theme, it is perhaps in the voicing of these 'invisible' voices – of writers from disinherited or suppressed social and ethnic backgrounds – that the Lyric has found its ally in linguistic innovation. The poets gathered in this anthology range across continents and are varied in terms of cultural backgrounds, gender and political persuasions; resulting in a selection quite different from the often-criticised emotional outpourings (and here we may read 'neo-Romantic' into those Projectivist-inspired criticisms of the Lyric) of the privileged Lyric 'I' from dominant (and often patriarchal) literary groupings.

Robert Sheppard, one of the UK's exponents of linguistically innovative poetry, has recently written of the need for writing that challenges, what he calls 'Empirical Lyricism':

> ...the solitary figure approaches an object or person with awe, only to be deflected or disappointed, before strategic withdrawal and some minute change in the narrator's belief systems. It is the blueprint for thousands of post-war poems.'[14]

Citing Philip Larkin's 'Whitsun Weddings' as the archetypal Empirical Lyric, Sheppard's critique points us to a subtext in which writers might purposefully innovate within their poetic traditions, for radical ends.[15] Sheppard's call for a deliberate writerly change – one that is required to engage with new problems of experience *in poetry* – leads us away from narrow senses of the poem as a record of empirical experience into an interest in the very processes of writing and the workings of language itself. Larkin himself made, it seems to me, the rather self-defeating claim that

> I write poems to preserve things I have seen / thought / felt (if I may so indicate a composite and complex experience), both for myself and for others, though I feel my prime responsibility is to the experience itself, which I am trying to keep from oblivion for its own sake.

which contains the seeds of its own negation: Larkin himself acknowledging that it is barely possible to 'so indicate a composite and complex experience... for others' *in language*. In other words, there is a problematic gap between *what* we experience and *how* we describe that experience; a gap that the project of Modernism made it one of its major concerns to address. Larkin, on the other hand chose to dismiss it, rather privileging his own idealised self with its set of – what seem at the start of the twenty-first century – reactionary social views.

I would like to contend then, that it is in this 'gap' that the interesting rubbing of shoulders between 'traditional' and 'innovative' has taken place. Lyric poetry has become more than an expression of musical subjectivity hoping to broaden its reference to universal experience; it has in fact come to explore the gaps between *the world as we experience it* and *experience as we describe it*. It is in this arena – that 'plot of land' between experience and the poem as experience – that the poets in this volume are also oftentimes writing. It is also within one of Lyric poetry's other traditions – that of measure: of breath, of phrase, of rhythm, of voice, of stanza, and more – that these poets also find their own, plural voices.

3. Poets (plural)

In his delightful and infamous twist to the original motto of the United States, *E Pluribus Unum* ('From the Many, One'), the American fiction writer David Foster Wallace wrote in *E Unibus Plurum: Television and US Fiction*[16] that future literary innovators might be prepared to turn their backs on irony and sarcasm and embrace, instead, 'untrendy human troubles and emotions'.

In doing so, the new rebels of writing might '…eschew hip fatigue, challenge the tyranny of irony, appear sincere… [and risk] accusations of sentimentality … of softness.'

Foster Wallace's yearning for the un-ironic partly can be traced into a feeling that, in our post-ironic world, one worthwhile task of writing might just be to seek a notion of 'truth' in an age of outrageous political spin, bare-faced lying over international conflicts, and a general feeling of debased cultural commodification. Famous for his ironic fiction, amongst other notable qualities, David Foster Wallace was, of course, being deadly ironic, or ironically serious. Now, some fifteen years on from his essay, we still live in a deadly ironic world; a world that is *supposedly* post '9/11'; post 'War on Terror'; post 'War on Drugs'; post 'War-on-whatever-you-want-to-wage-a-war-against'; post-Balkans; post-Diana; post-Rwanda; post-Painting; post-AIDS; post Postmodernism; post everything. Simply, 'Post'. And, arguably, 'post' none of those things for, in the very act of identifying them as 'Post-' again and again, we ironically never get beyond them, until iconoclasm, neglect, or simple forgetfulness consign them to the 'past'. What is a poet to do?

The poets of this anthology risk accusations of sorts, simply because they dare to write lyric poems in an age when, in the late twentieth century at least, the Lyric has taken a considerable bashing.[17] Given the excitement of these poets' work (amongst the work of many other new and established writers who are pushing at manifold lyric boundaries – poetic-cultural-political-spiritual-aesthetic-sexual-racial and so on), I think that that bashing is quite unjust. These writers are able to fuse old and new strategies to explore what contemporary notions of truth (of sincerity) might be, even when being sincerely ironic. They may borrow from Romanticism as much as from the innovative traditions of OuLiPo or L=A=N=G=U=A=G=E poets, and are aware of the post-Romantic dissolution and uncertainty of the self, as much as the Romantic search for the ideal self. These poets are aware that all strategies have their time, place and function. As David Kennedy so astutely wrote in an earlier edited volume of mine, *Binary Myths*

> In terms of poetic practice, poetry is not a choice between ellipsis and parataxis or metaphor and simile, but a recognition that not only are all four valuable strategies, but that none are either exclusively avant garde or exclusively mainstream.[18]

In realising this through their poems, these writers pull off surprising, sometimes daring (and sometimes quietly unassuming) acts of Lyric balance. They are also able to position themselves in terrains of, what often appear to be, mutually contradictory states, yet still retaining their integrity. I respect these choices to assimilate and digest strategies from a broad spectrum: if we have moved on culturally into post-Postmodernism, then from its metaphoric 'big bang' new orders must surely be emerging from its debris. I hope this anthology represents one possible part of that underground network of creative energies: here are Lyric poets in the formal sense, but they are also prose poets, experimental poets, performance poets, spirited poets, innovative poets, humorous poets, social-realist poets, political poets, personal poets, traditionalists *and* avant-gardistes. They are, actually, like all of us who strive to do it well (and we forget this at our peril, theorising and criticism aside), quite simply good poets worth reading.

This is not a manifesto; neither theirs, nor mine. What I hope this anthology risks (in place of the didactic thrust and canon making of many such volumes) is sincerity, as much as it celebrates irony; it eschews 'hip fatigue' just as it embraces softness. It is, I believe, a collection of poems that understands and demonstrates that innovation within the Lyric can only ever have meaning in relation to the diverse traditions of the Lyric, in whichever patch of ground those traditions might have seeded, sprouted and grown towards the light of readership. The traditions of these poets are, like their personal and cultural backgrounds, plural. Their experiments, where they exist, are hybrid. *E unibus plurum*: from the One, Many. As that quote so simply achieves, these poets invert our notions of expectation and, as the Lyric has always done, I believe the results of their explorations sing.

As with the real, hands-on allotment, where generations of working people have momentarily escaped the realities of modern urban living to cultivate something of their own and of themselves, the 'tracts' of these Lyric poems are spaces within which cultivation and growth figure strongly. And, as with the other meaning of 'allotment' – that 'measure', 'share', or 'quota' – these poets can only ever be a portion of the diverse make-up of the contemporary Lyric and, as such, a representation of my own tastes and interests within that diversity. Some of them I have been lucky enough to tutor and mentor in recent years. The work of others I first discovered in journals, anthologies and early collections. In each case I have been moved and impressed by their talent and quiet integrity, amidst the hoo-hah and clamour of the annual big prizes, and the publicity rounds of Generations 'New-', 'Next-', 'Whenever-' and 'Never-'. All deserve a wider, appreciative audience and readership. I sincerely hope (and may I so appear, sincere, Mr. Foster Wallace?) this anthology serves them well in that endeavour.

Andy Brown, 2005

NOTES

1 Jon Cook's excellent *Poetry in Theory 1900- 2000* (Blackwells, 2004) collects these articles and others and provides a wide-ranging survey of the relevant critical positionings for those interested in tracing the development of critical debates in modern poetry and poetics.

2 Wallace Stevens, from *The Idea of Order at Key West*

3 *Strong Words: modern poets on modern poetry*, eds, Herbert & Hollis (Bloodaxe Books, 2000)

4 The metaphor of the 'rhizome', is extensively developed in Deleuze and Guattari's major work, *A Thousand Plateaus: Capitalism and Schizophrenia* [University of Minnesota Press, 1987]. The definition of 'rhizome' I find particularly pleasing for the context of my metaphoric 'allotment': a rhizome is an underground, horizontal stem from which roots, tubers and branches arise (for example, potatoes and grasses). Rhizomes are regenerative and spreading and support complex networks of modular plant units, sustaining growth across a wide distribution.

5 T.S. Eliot, in *The Sacred Wood* (1920) (London: Faber, 1997) pp. 105-6. Eliot goes on to distinguish between echoing, imitating and plagiarising.

6 In her volume *Reading Paul Muldoon* (Bloodaxe 1998), Claire Wills discusses this problem of novelty and repetition in relation to Muldoon's poem 'The Little Black Book' (from *Hay*, Faber & Faber 1998). Wills specifies a problem in this poem that might be generalised to a wider body of avant garde writers, noting how '…here apparent novelty looks a lot like tedious reduplication, variety is difficult to distinguish from monotony.' Claire Wills, p195

7 Kurt Schwitters used the techniques of collage, most notably in a work with the letters MERZ in red capitals torn from the advertisement of a Bank (*Commerz und Privatbank*). From this he described his later assemblages as *Merz*.

8 The *New Princeton Encyclopaedia of Poetry and Poetics* states that, 'Although lyric poetry is not music, it is representative of music in its sound patterns, basing its meter and rhyme on the regular linear measure of the song; or, more remotely, it employs cadence and consonance to approximate the tonal variation of a chant or intonation.' p715

9 *The New Princeton Encyclopedia of Poetry and Poetics*, Princeton University Press, 1993, p714. This volume contains a detailed essay on the origin, definitions, historical and contemporary developments of the lyric.

10 *The Poet's Point of View*, Basil Bunting

11 *The New Princeton Encyclopedia of Poetry and Poetics*, p726

12 Carol Ann Duffy's poem, 'Mrs. Midas', was perhaps one that spawned a whole 'mini-tradition' of such poems, later stretching to Duffy's whole collection of this type of poem, *The World's Wife*

13 *The New Princeton Encyclopedia of Poetry and Poetics* , p726

14 Robert Sheppard, informal article / private correspondence

15 See Sheppard's 'The Education of Desire' in his collection of articles and essays, *Far Language* (Stride)

16 from David Foster Wallace, *A Supposedly Fun Thing I'll Never Do Again*, 1990

17 Again, the reader might like to see Jon Cook's *Poetry in Theory* for excerpts of Projectivist and other Poststructural arguments against the Lyric.

18 David Kennedy in *Binary Myths*, ed. Andy Brown (Stride, 1998)

Avik Chanda

Memory-Triptych
for Ulrike

I

In a comparison of infinities, God,
my chief obsession, takes first place –
and so my churchgoing in Cologne.
I have not seen my own Gods.
Yet, between the aisle and the altar
between the organ and its codex
I have spotted His Old Testament-profile
primeval and dark like a draught
forbidding and unforgiving
like so many of my own.

II

2:30 a.m. Winter. And a walk
in the snow. The silence
of blue crunch phosphorescing underfoot.
At the crossing, dwarfing the traffic lights
a strange translucence in the sky, that
had the feel of morning windscreens
cold and crusty: a rub of the thumb
would produce a crack, the wipers
clear the frost, and I look
through it, beyond the void.

III

You, my empfindliche late October,
you were there (and here I speak of
the present as if you were my past),
my andante sunset, as when
the violinist tunes his instrument,
creating a note that is not part of his score
and therefore transcendental – you were
my moment when the Gods had withdrawn,
after granting a spell of off-season snow,
and only the pain remained, my thaw.

Malevich

I

In the end, there was only white
The canvas, too,
stripped to its bare minimum
frame
perfect square.
Three coats of paint, opaque,
smooth as skeins.
In it, garbled forms dance
shapes that are dreamed of
that do not exist
streams of infinite colours
reaped by phosphorus

II

And how would I ever,
having reached this,
what is certainly a dead end,
return?
And how shall I
make virtues of dead blocks
stolid buildings
purpled distances lined with blue
the colour of loss?
To paint figures again,
women aged before their time
pregnant, starving,
but always falsely muscular
always these ridiculous fists raised.

III

Then there were the nights
while wind and ice raged outside
like tortured stars.
In bed, disarranged
over the sheets
the eyes that could still speak
know still the value
of what had been lost.
A late photograph.

IV

Praised be the absence of content over the
Praised be the absence of colour over
Praised be the absence of consciousness over the
Praised be the absence of shape over

There shall be no texture
There shall be no form
There will be no

V

In the end, there was only light.

Torch Lamp Drawings

I

A neat triangle at first, equilateral,
as in the Vastusutra, then another,
inverted and superimposed on it,
and at the bottom, craggy letters
in Bengali: fire, water, life –
the desperate refuse of hope.

II

Thin strokes strung in a mesh
around the wishing tree: Puri.
Here, for a hundred or two,
we guarantee riches and sons
and a laptop job. Tie your string,
my good sir, like the others.

III

Lively at the *Nacht den Museen*:
a clot of mellow light at the top
left-hand corner, with lines
sliding down in beered perspective,
tracing a lithograph tracing Böll:
der Zug war punktlich

IV

Dermis over veins, blood, flesh
and metacarpals. Her hand.
And between the sunburnt here
and there of skin, this most
delicate of all strokes, marking
the band where she wore her ring.

Histories

I

Wood a million years old,
long timed to stone, now lying on its flank
in an empty porch, where on
undisturbed afternoons, crows perch
to spread their chalk. And to think
I almost fell off it once,
as a child, tightwalking its length.

II

From here, you hear the guide saying,
you only see the tip of the palace.
Underneath, the king's favourite
dreams up her body as a lake,
blue to the touch, and the light,
festering at the surface,
plays in her vault like shoals.

III

Footfalls in an old lane. Rain washes
down a slope towards the building.
At the entrance, a gargoyle,
leper-mouthed, screams inaudibly
at the unexpected visitor,
who hurriedly folds his umbrella
and steps into the dark.

IV

A moment of sublime distraction,
when, as in that ancient dusk,
the Tirthankar inhabits the smile
in his own bust,
but only for a moment,
leaving the stone
vacant and blind like a child.

V

And to feel that I am all these
and many more, older things –
swords, armies, dust in sunlight,
a stone in rigor, carved
and polished to perfection,
in turn broken, but kept ticking,
waiting for oblivion.

Divinities

Cupids, even the grotesquely fat ones,
inevitably show off when photographed,
waving flowers and curls, lips puckered
in a daintier-than-stucco pout.
Angels, however, are a different matter.

Waiting through an eternity
of distant sculpted smiles, in torpor,
black or broken winged, ripped in turn
to bare shell wounds or the scourge,
they bear the mark of Cain.

There are those in hiding, darkly,
till the floodlight bursts in on them
from atop a crowded monument - and
for an instant you see the beaten profile,
an eye irisless, where acid had lashed the face.

And those living among us incognito -
the girl you asked for change
at the railway station, feeling
the brush of light in her fingers -
whom we are yet to discover.

Humayun's Tomb

Each time you close your eyes,
you look up a sheen of swords.
Where their hilts meet, light climbs
the palm of the dome; pigeons
animate an irrevocable time.
Then a swarm of horses casts
after-images on your retina,
surrounding the façade stone-scratched
with heart-signs and lovers' names:
you hear their hooves in the wind's ear.
The arches bend and grey like
the king who sheltered here when
everything was lost, thinking:
in this place, I shall be safe,
my spirits will protect me.
The breath of guns and traitors
swims up like shapes in the heat.

Now you may open your eyes:
they are all still there.

Nabami

I

Heat, during the day,
the view shimmering
as if seen through flames.

The leaf that twirled
into my palm
burns in the sacred fire.

Wood and cloth crackle
where fire and water meet,
sand rustling. Dissolve.

II

Incense and the dance of lights;
The priest, swaying to the beat of drums
wakes in his dream, to the Goddess,

lofty and unapproachable,
and therefore alive – a smile
visible through the smoke.

Hands that have held me
now fold in prayer.
Cut to

III

The night. Longshot.
Echoes of drums
silent in the distance.

The city, dimpled with pandal-hoods.
They throw off
parabolic nets of light

into the sky, focii meeting
at a point beyond –
Three-Eyed.

Abi Curtis

The Allotment

Look for it here:

follow the black-berried track to where
shallots and violets reek their invites.

Unlock the gate that breaks the morning's
spider's web, letting
parsnip tips receive their droplets.

These boots, forever moulded to your toes,
stand in line with queues of rhubarb.

Gently brush the furled kale,
fall in love with veined greengages:
rain bubbles solidified

to flesh, their globular heads
amongst the buttered lettuce.

Wigwams of lanky broad beans,
white-hot, red-dipped radishes,
muscled spinach give

as you lift the mole-black soil
and ease them to your barrow.

You will not find the answer here

Or in the quick flick of a rabbit's tail,
startled by its own curved image
in the pendulous drag of damsons.

Or in uneven squares of plots,
dapper scarecrows, copper taps,

or in the field below the slope
where year-old horses chase
themselves along the fences.

For there is nothing of it here.

You can watch a marrow loom
from lithe courgette
to grotesque thumb,

or pull apart an artichoke:
one tubular heart, one bulbous choke.

But look close

along your sun-dried arm,
your nails bedded with wet earth,
the flaked handle of a trowel or fork

twisting in the mulch and worms.
Find, among each sift and turn;

walk-less husks of millipedes
and unforgiving knots of weed;
this is where you'll learn.

A Power Cut

stopped short our quarrel.
You were mid-vowel, your eyes wide,
I was consoling the last of the bottle.
A loss of shadows brought
silence and a cryptic table-top.

How many matches have we got?
Two, I think, and a crooked candle.

They made an amber island of our table.

Strange objects moved their angles on our shelves,
as though at night-time they had other selves.
Your arms: alive with optic-down,
half of you enhanced, the other: gone.
Shall we talk? I asked, and reached across,
mistaking your hand for the honey pot.

Abode

I have a home that breathes
into its blue garden, asking leave.

I have a home that breathes,
as a melting ice-cube shifting
off its droplets, slowly shrinking
into its blue garden, asking leave.

As a melting ice-cube shifting,
my home is thinking; its corners clatter
with a thousand knotted matters;
like droplets, slowly shrinking.

My home is thinking; its corners clatter –
the scent of basil and the fraying threads,
whispers of letters, yawns of empty beds:
a thousand knotted matters.

The scent of basil and the fraying threads,
boxes of time and solitude,
days spent warming rooms and fixing grooves,
whispers of letters, yawns of empty beds.

Boxed in by time and solitude,
it stirs and rips the roots of its square foot. It's standing,
shaking off the dreams of worms, deciding to abandon
days spent warming rooms and fixing grooves.

It stirs and rips the roots of its square foot. It's standing.
Trailing mud across the shingles,
it lummoxes through town, its new life tingles,
shaking off the dreams of worms, deciding to abandon.

Trailing mud across the shingles,
it blows the ashes from its chimney,
and makes a plan to live out in the forest, like a yeti.
Far from town, a new life tingles.

It blows the ashes from its chimney,
finds a clearing and some pleasant birches,
fills itself with squirrels, ivies, chaffinch-perches,
lives forever in the forest like a yeti.

I had a home that breathed
into its blue garden, asking leave.

It's blown the ashes from its chimney,
is living in the forest, like a yeti.

Hong Kong

I was a gwailo, waiting on the harbour-front, buttoned-up in itchy green. No doubt, the sweat drawing its way down my starched collar smelt to others of milk and butter. Junks dunked in the brown water, lit up from above by dragons of neon. Evil spirits were being dashed off feng shui buildings, deflected into the sweet stench of the South China, smoothed over by the ferry-man. The sweep of the science building was a cornet of shells. I looked into a window, transparent blue. The same colour as my eyes. And saw you, leaning to the light, standing in the lab, coated in white; a sanitised angel. You squinted at glass tubes, held them up to the dropping dim sum of the sun; little phials of gold liquid. I had journeyed all my life to see this: your flat frown through a window. I had been a thin white dog, lost within the cardboard streets of the walled city. I had walked the Des Voeux Road, meeting pith-helmeted men in the Old Gloucester Hotel, breathing the rot of blue eggs boiled behind doorways. I had lived with Salisbury Row's clammy touches to my silver buttons, stumbling across Blake Pier, coming up for air to watch ladders rise from the water. All for this: my feet crossing from Tsim Sha Tsui, you viewing the urine samples of strangers, catching my stare and flicking the blinds shut. My lungs felt bashed by a cricket bat.

But later, as the spores began to swell in their humid petri-dish, you sought me out with my sun-burnt scalp, taking my arm, trying your mouth on stretched English vowels. We found our scrap of gold along Nathan Road, and kept a stone frog at the windowsill. That way, we stayed together when the little red book went off like a bomb, laying low 'til Deng swept in with the monsoons, washing everything in side-ways rain.

In time, the plane takes us out, touching cheongsams drying on the precarious threads between buildings. The city expands hourly into the sky, and it takes time to climb high enough to leave . You've never seen the clouds like this: clean. To you, they have been scrubbed and softly brushed. They are all around us now, resting on the hills. They smell of pine and rabbits' fur.

On the Level

Stooping to pick up a sock,
little arrows of sunlight at my back,
I put some muscle out in my neck
with the terrible twang of an elastic band
slinging off its duty.
And, ever since, I've been unable
to move my head to the right.
Instead, I've become android,
turning my torso to sound,
living on a swivel chair.
It puts me in mind of my grandfather,
his past life as a carpenter,
now nine years in the clinic.
Rich with wrinkles,
polishing the corridors with charm.
He's perfect, except he walks tilted,
magnetised by the left-hand side.
Tipped to the limit, he strides,
unaware that my brain bends as I watch.
The doctor videoed and played him back.
'It's because of your Parkinsons.'
He gaped, flat hands sawing the chair-arms.
'I thought I walked straight'.
His body, in age, pays no mind
to angles or lines,
grumbles stubbornly at gravity.
He shuts himself in the workshop for days.
I worry, tipping my ear to the door,
listening as wood chips and fizzes under his hands.
He emerges, smelling of burnt mosses,
proudly holding a pair of glasses,
on which hangs a spirit-level.
Its bubble trembles as he rests them on his nose.

He lunges for the corridor,
arrows pointing reality,
narrowing down the last days.
I watch him, losing sight
as he turns right.

Parallel Universe

Separated at birth, un-twinned and living parallel,
their DNA, magnetised, tugging at each other's universe.

The one married and paralysed
with the nine to five. The other at university

obsessed with anatomy, to be a paramedic:
Robin Hood in an ambulance, always unjoined

from his other, wandering on the bubbled parameter
of a 'maybe he'll need me someday and we'll meet'. Unjustly,

they never would. Possibility played paramour
to some other pair of twins, one dapper, the other unkempt,

meeting on Oprah for the first time, paranoid
about their just-met mirror, unkindly

showing themselves to themselves. The paranormal
of their own ghosts, the knowable unknowables

of the overgrown lost roads , the parapet
bulldozed and the twiny knots of roots unlaced

to show the not-so-them with all its paraphernalia
of other paths, plastered to them, so unladylike,

blasted in too-bright light, holding a parasol,
sewn from scraps of difference. The gate of somewhere else unlatched,

to deliver like a fifty-year-old parcel
those things they could have unleashed.

Rose Flint

Above Saint Cybi's Well

Saint Cybi's ravens are seeing-off marauding herring-gulls
in a black/white war inside the wind above the towering beech trees.
I'd always cast the seagulls as the bad guys, it's those hooked-back
prehistoric wings like flick-knives and how they've threatened me
in seaside alleys where the deli's leaving spilt an easy crust.

And seagulls have no wisdom myths attached like leashes to their legs,
connecting threads that tie us bird to human heart. Seagulls are always bird
and alien, but Raven speaks our many-storied tongue: their druid voice
prophesies approaching death and rain that brings resurgence,
Raven is our helpful spirit-guide, our guardian and healer and Raven
is the Morrigan's vicious wartime pet that feasts on dying sight.
Ravens are one-eyed Odin's seers, Memory and Thought
and Raven is the Trickster. Only anonymous long-drowned sailors
are shut inside a seagull's head; you can see them glare out resentfully
through those sea-cold yellow eyes, always fathoms under.

Raucous, elegant, the ravens float and wheel, returning to their roost.
There's good pickings for them here, I count a dozen sheep skulls
whiter than the loaves of quartz that build the lowest walls of ancient huts
half-lost beneath the gorse. Enough to feed a family
nine times over nine. Here, in this high place, wind starves against stone
and the silver-sheeted sea is hammered over distance by the cold
to lie as still as death or enchantment, and as devious. *Oh love,*
who told you it was better to stumble blindly up the mountain to die alone
than to stay and fight for another hour in the raw beauty of the air?

Sometimes it seems that nothing has a plan. It's all tumbled anyhow,
like this mossy rockfall, like those dead brown leaves
rolled inside the heart's cave of a striped-out ewe's carcass,
like the moody sea. I can't answer any of the questions.
I can only watch patterns forming in the air as the great black birds
soar and swoop the edge of life searching out the little hunted deaths,
the failures of breath or mothering.
If I stay here longer miracles of warm sun and basking snakes might happen
or I could freeze forever into the wheezy hollow of my hurting chest
where my energy is turning into dust. Either way,
there will still be ravens here, nesting in tall trees, shadow wingspans
circled on the wind. Yesterday I did not see
the way their presence altered light. Nor what would heal me.

Vixen

             I could put my hands over my ears
but the sound is too white   blurred high-frequency
                   howling
and is inside me anyway   so what
             could I keep out?   As if the breath of a vixen
had filtered into my room's black night air
when I was sleeping
                   so I am tuned now
             to cunning, doubling back, sleight of hand, light
and edge of shadow   this running fox
       with her masks and seven selves –
                   that's how she hunts her freedom,
the hot guise of fur's dark stole over bare shoulders
             dancing stilettos. And I have four puppety-limbs
             and a puppety-heart jiggling in space
because fox isn't there, not there in the real.
       in the grief-place   she's out thieving
             testing the cut-throat sing of the wires
       one more time. She will only enter
the black hole inside her in extremis of love. Loving her children
licking their baby roly-poly arms, one side a delicate fur
biscuit-cindered by sun, the other as sweet and white
as bread; softness so deep she kisses, she nuzzles
                   and rolls in it, rubs her face in its bliss. Then she must
                   race to the stream, river, lake or wherever
                   will take the terrible stink of love away
so no one will know, ever
where to find the cave of her heart   that holds them
always safe.   So she goes
threading her way back nervously between thistles
       and thorn trees and ice, a red line of blood
             tailing out of her
anyway   the hounds already here.

Domestic Goddess

It is not in the instances of chocolate parfait
that I become a Domestic Goddess,
nor within the bain-marie nor the couscous.
            No, rather it is in the spaces
after housework – the kind that comes
three weeks late and shows in low sun's freight
of dust motes like stellar atoms
suspended in a dance over dulled furniture
                    – in these spaces
when my orderliness has polished the shine
into gold frames and chestnut surfaces,
when china sings with all its mouths
clean and wide open as nests full of thrushes
and glass celebrates itself in mirrors of light
then – when I am alone
and float through the presences of every room
blessing things gently – this clock of ages,
these pages and sweet cakes
                then I grow tall and svelte
dress in rivery silvery gowns and stilettos
make my mouth a wild luscious mulberry
trail musk over the windows in veils
and trap the street sounds like flies for slaughter
so the bright silence will sing me
and you will respond
in each room's bloom and dizziness
will bow and give thanks and follow me
into the white linen sanctum upstairs
where the windows are wide to the oak spires
and birds robed as black priestesses, sing praise.

Grace

How I fear the ice that comes like a midnight thief
to smother my heart when cold winter
is more than weather and Time is snapped in its stalk.

Old Winter: the two-faced woman who bears such
deathly features and such grace as she walks
towards me, comes to turn my unwilling face to her gaze

and I see the world shrink to the target's eye, gold hawk
flung in a fire to raze all the patterns that are beautiful,
so we are lost. Our futures as poor as dust.

In this hour Vixen creeps from the hole, screams
her nightmare song in my dream of tomorrow stark
as snow, a long forever white-out without kindness.

But she is singing the coming months into new life
and being wholly alive, grace is as necessary as the flow
of blood or water. I listen: Winter marks me, makes me

know that in the terror of loss, the iron seizure of frost –
grace still holds strong as light: fox-star in the dark.
Believing then in grace is good enough: is grace itself.

Gallt y Widdan
Hill of the Witch

Has she gone into the wary heron
that pleats her great feather cloak
into stillness and stands
wings of slate and her stone headstalk
carefully pivoting, all the awareness
of river's jade, river's citrine,
river's dark quartz
in her black avid eye, kindled blade beak?

Or has she fled gently into the blue smoke
of the bells or the bride-white blackthorn?
(Needlethorns longer than thin fingers,
sharp, dangerous to the heart.)
Is she here in the guise of a fly?
Does she lie in the snake's tight bed
of bracken, or the blue egg
or the spotted snake's head fritillary?
Has she shifted
into the young black bull stamping the juices
from crushed green garlic and wild violets?
Is she crouched in sorrel's white star?

She is here,
speaking under the river's raucous voice:
Listen to me, listen, listen to me...
She is stone, she is water, she is wren,
she is the wind and her breath lifts my hair
as her presence slides over my skin.

Faiths

You are looking for something to recognise
but the altar is recessed in darkness, black cave-mouth
roaring and smoking with gilt and incense

Saints stare plaintively out, bleeding from the powers
of their silvers and oil and jewels; like survivors
we stumble into the courtyard of wide white air

high as the lammergeirs; there is one pomegranate tree
dressed like a dancing woman in fire-red silk:
skirts deep enough to burn your lips.

At Armeni you photograph me under the kerm oaks:
I am a priestess serving the spirits with my hands
of dry leaves and jade lizards.

You lean down to take the picture from me as I stand
in the stark angle of the dromos; in the shadow behind me
the Goddess is axle, stone pillar of light.

You retreat to wait on a bank of wild narcissus
where you are Pan, playing gospels on your pipe
careful as a Jain of the small lives of beetles

as you talk to the goats in the same soft chattering
swooping bird-speech that the lemon-leaf-gathers
call to each other across the groves.

I feel the breath of the cold stones at my back as beautiful.
When I turn round, the sun itself
is your kiss on the nape of my neck.

Fire Hare

I saw a brown hare in the wheatfield
   long ears pointed to the sun
like two sweetcorns of fire   blazing out

       Late summer air has thinned:
frail as organza this sheen it plays
briefly, over us.   Without these mirrors
how would we see   the touch of fire
goldenness   all that is numinous

here?   We may only have   one moment
like the gilded hare   and if all else is dross
      I am also this

Thoth, when you weigh my heart
know that I have only come lately to sun
and these things my heart carries lightly
    as a heron feather   grey as rain.

Iain Galbraith

Skew

A day *full derke* and slanting rain in ropes
Hung from the sky, its gabled cloud as always sealed
The soft stone terre-à-terre.

I turned to the opening west and saw
Those bands of shadow drawn across the grey beyond
The water's mass evanishing in air.

As if against indifference their firmer hue
Arose behind the river mouth – that fjord, channel,
Sound, the straits of anywhere:

A little row of flats, the transverse
Gradients of waves were cables taut between their posts,
And still the sky remained – a shield, the arch obscure.

The Voice

The man was half
A mile long, tipping the dunes
To the fluted fields.

Behind him the sun
Long-legged, discreet
Stalked the jagged rocks.

The lazy-beds stretched
Pink beneath the skirts
Of the ingoing squall

And a flock of plover
Starved for a week, gorged
On the thawing land.

Turned-to for an instant
Lost, a hailing voice
Far out to sea.

A Brim of Lather on the Bay of Cologne

The day shrank like a *pulli*
    In the roaring sky of your absence in the rattling rage

Of the rain the black bag scraped the brickwork sparring
    With the magpies for the branch-space in our pine

I read my Magda Tulli
    Then watched the rooks and startled clouds engage

In feats of daring till my wheels locked on the water kissing
    The kerb of loss and spinning into early middle age

The explorative mouse at once resumed its labours
    While you in clarity crossed the swollen theory of the Rhine

Ach by now you'll be skirting the hoary cliffs of Vane
    The vantage of Vorlich the snow-capped Boulders of Narnain

To gain your ring-road and the walnut patch of grey
    On the rumps of tired fieldfares on a branch in passage

To the marbled south you stream as though through corridors
    That thread the Bulge for Biscay where each gust

Whips your horse higher over brims of lather on the Bay
    So look down will you at the stain

White on the legs of a piano we failed to shift upstairs in time
    We've survived the flood sure but the wind has brought

The sour rot of apples from some corner we'd love to remain
    This Baroque palace fouled by the feral papingo

Passing the Steading

If tups and fank are all but ghosts
the void they haunt is living earth:
The way damp worsted rubbed on stone
or shapes we work dissolve in rain.

Matisse of the North

for Heiko Linnemann

The pink roof caves in with all things folded and cracked.
Slowly at first to the east it crumbles from a peeling corner
bleeding to the skirting that has already smudged: a gashed
cavern, its Doric columns lifting the temple of interior blue.
This was made by Henri Matisse, recumbent on his golden
quilt, flushed and trembling with cold, his tall brush-strokes
tracing distant script on a ceiling that has not ceased to shift.
The seconds halt as a V drips into the frost-bound sedge.
There are charred slashes left and right on the face of what is
also your sky, the copse of blackest green. Leaving this space
you will notice the voluble cloud, how surprisingly small
and low it lies at the water's edge, beckoning across the sand.

Wych Hazel

Milk floods the hollow
moating the lower copse.

Then you come in reaching for the salt loop
gleaming on the arm of an overnight lagoon.

It was but a short visit.
Thirty steps down the mist has already drained
the iron-age mound
rising to the centre of the field.

Bubbles in a frond of seaweed
rooks, whirling
waters over stunted elms

it's gone

stonechat

Hacking into Forever

'How can a soul be a merchant? What relation to an immortal
being have the price of linseed, the fall of butter ...'
  – Walter Bagehot

A glacial pass led me down to the middle
where spent salmon lay in rows in the shallows of a lake,
bruised souls. No cry was heard

the day I torched the tomes of Atlanta – *Brachyura*,
mute hermit crabs, recall the act. *Nyassa*,
Poseidonia, La Nouvelle Caledonie – there is no end

to the work of erasure. For see my eyeless lovers shine
and all our children and their children's offspring
gather on the roofs. In search of myself I enter the Eocene.

Hortus Conclusus
for Màiri

Her reflection inclosed bathing molten and blue
Flowers without a shadow: now the weeping child
Will sleep and the glinting heads of my floorboard nails
Climb through the timber sky.

Echo

The *plat* sea lacking a chargeable event

     swells

          beneath

          the claw-red, cellulite sky

but me leaving you is leaving me
     a candle spill by the swimming-pool.

Once again

          dinner-jackets chequer the patio. They
               whisper euros to the cracked azure.

The Wait

These pages filled now turning to my left
I stare across the room and out a window
Into space that ends it's said with apertures
On other rooms and slips their hold through glass
To lose all contour in the grey, and am bereft
Of all but ins and outs and spaces in between
As she stands there and stretches in a dress
Unworn for forty years, so pale, so late
Against the streaming clouds her white hair
Blackens on the plate of sky, and when
She lifts an arm to wave its fabric shores
The bay, and that is why I bring her here
And there is nothing we can do but wait.

Luke Kennard

Film Noir

Broken shadows through Venetian blinds.
'This has the soft note of improvisation,'
I said, 'our dialogue.' She missed her cue.

The bell-boy signalled with his fez,
Hissing unhelpful *non-sequiturs* down his sleeve.
She shrugged, eyes wide – which sufficed.

'This has the sickening note of a play seen drunk,'
I said, 'forgotten laughter and obliterated space.'
'And what do I have to do for a cigarette?' she said.

The director was busy with his Freudian tarot cards;
Sometimes metal dice would fall out of his pocket:
'Hey mister, you dropped some change... oh.'

I'm scuppered: the way the silhouettes play on her dress;
The metre of her footsteps in the hall;
The nervous flowers drawn on the backs of her hands.

•

After hours I go walking with the shooting script,
Ignoring whispers from freshly dug alley-ways,
'Hey, buddy, want to come check out the darkness

I just excavated?' My wisecracks don't add up
In bare interiors – they are shattered by a stammer –
So I smile in a parody of genuine warmth

Which, time and again, is misconstrued
As genuine warmth – by myself as much as others.
Nobody takes their tears more seriously

Than a man who never cries. Another monogrammed
Handkerchief: of course, when you *follow*,
You end up exactly where they want you.

.

I do not recognise the handwriting of my putative friend;
Have I been telling jokes in my sleep again?
'Bad ones,' she confirms, nodding.

.

The director is bed-ridden by the thought of bad reviews;
Plenty of his enemies are free-lance writers.
I wait, smoking in the cavities of the set.

'I tapped a stranger's shoulder; I was looking for you,'
I explain to the shadow of a vase behind a pillar.
Later I go calling her name around the docks

Until a window opens in a tall building
And I cover my ears, running for home.
This is more, you understand, than a professional concern.

.

Leaving the industry party I saw a smile
Which turned out to be my reflection
In the lustre of the balustrade.

That night I hear she vanished in a yellow cab
To the wild applause of the rain –
I was making toast at the time of the call.

When we finally broke down her door we found
A white curtain flapping in the open window –
As if waving goodbye.

The Tree

I was arrested for writing of a tree I didn't care about. The tree represented me in court all the same. It must have really loved me.

'Ladies and gentlemen,' said the tree, 'I implore you to consider how senseless this case is. If this man did not love me, nay, cared nothing for me at all, what would posses me to stand here today vouching for his character?'

'Objection!' cried the prosecution. 'The tree is speculating.'

'Sustained,' muttered the judge. 'Get to the point, tree.'

The only witness was an old man with a bad leg who had seen me writing an ode in the park whilst eating a baguette.

'He had an expression on his face,' said the old man, 'I don't know, though... But there was definitely an expression on his face while he sat there, chewing and scribbling. I don't know, though.'

'Would you consider calling it a *cynical expression*?' said the prosecution.

'Objection,' said the tree, with practised insouciance. 'Leading the witness.' The tree really was a class act.

But Autumn fell, and with it the tree's silence – and my hearing was postponed until March. But by then the tree had forgotten all about me and the trial. It explained to the jury that it stored its memories in its leaves; 'Much like a human stores its memories in its brain.'

The tree delivered a moving closing statement about time and wisdom – and the colour of rust and the light breeze in the corner of a pasture.

Nevertheless, I was found guilty of negligence, fined £3,700 and banned from writing about trees for the rest of my Earthly tenure.

Glass

Darkness – and the moths converge
To flick themselves against the mesh,
As I compress the day's affairs
And write them out as epigrams:
In which our hero takes a bath
And talks obscenely to himself.

I'm staring at an unlit candle,
Thinking of a lit candle –
Which is no way to light a candle,
But a fine way of saving it.
You used to scratch your arms, but now
Nothing is wrong, my dearest one:
Your most horrible thoughts are just
The broken glass in an unbroken glass.

I am No Longer Your Pilot

A pig fell out of the sky.
It landed poorly, but was not wounded.
'Tell me,' said the pig, 'of cruelty;
Tell me of the sweet, stale smoke on your fingertips;
Tell me of your tinnitus and your unsightly body hairs.'

I heard a note that carried my will away
So instead I told the pig of obloquy and calumny,
And the pig was satisfied – which is no great stroke.
He slept a while, but presently awoke and squawked,
'Teach me of satire and upper-body strength.'

I was born under the space between two stars,
So instead I beat a military tattoo with maracas
And sang about national identity and gender.
But this time the pig was not satisfied.
'That is not what I asked for at all,' he complained.

'You have reneged on your promise.
You are no gentleman and have learned nothing
About yourself you did not already know.'
Now the pig was becoming transparent,
His form but condensation and mist.

I turned my back on the city.
I moved to a log cabin in Finland.
Where I never read magazines, just looked at the snow
And the silver light on the urns, and the pig-shaped absence.
I never shook off that pig-shaped absence.

Egalitarianism

Bitterly reviewing my old P.E. teacher's first collection of short stories,
Stories in which the narrator turns out in the last line to be an animal;
Stories in which a man dies mid sentence and is met by a loved one in
    the afterlife;
Stories in which characters keep saying, 'I need to talk to you', instead of
    actually fucking talking;
Stories in which a man stands on the edge of a cliff drearily
    contemplating suicide for 7,000 words;
Stories with dogs in them;
Stories in which nobody simply *enjoys* something when they could
    'Secretly delight in it';
Stories in which not one of the bit players can begin to comprehend the
    plight of the lead, such is the comparative paucity of their imagination;
Stories in which people calmly and deliberately blow their brains out
    with a service revolver,
As if one could calmly and *accidentally* blow one's brains out with a
    service revolver;
Drug stories in which a boy on acid falls out of a window;
Stories in which the main character has a headache;
Stories of trauma after trauma after trauma – in which 'Sandra couldn't
    believe it' and 'Doug just couldn't understand what had happened' and
    neither can the reader;
Stories in which something echoes or clatters or reverberates through
    somebody's mind, as if that means anything at all;
Stories in which people stand at the edge of the infinity of themselves;
Stories in which a bullied kid blows up the school;
Stories in which a man cannot understand his crazy son – ending on a
    sentimental, valedictory note of hope;
Metafictional stories about a writer who can't think of a good idea for a
    story;
Zany stories involving a monkey;
Moral stories about a man who had an affair – although we skip any of
    the juicy bits and cut straight to him sitting in his living room 10
    years later, wallowing in guilt;

Under-researched stories in which 'Lisa couldn't believe she'd got that
    job as a hotshot lawyer', but is then cast in a story where her cat dies
    and nothing else happens;
Stories involving long quotations from song lyrics to lend the piece sham
    profundity;
Risky, experimental stories that use long dashes instead of speech-marks
    to no effect whatsoever;
Hallmark love stories that you finish and no longer believe in love;
Heavily nuanced stories in which the metaphor for a failing marriage can
    be no less than their house burning down –
And one of the characters has to make reference to the symbol in
    dialogue, just in case anyone missed it.

Blue Dog

The blue dog is made of plastic. It is no more than two inches high. The blue dog is a pug and sits on its haunches. It is what she has been looking for all her life. 'You remember being a child, don't you?' she asks me.

This is what I remember about being a child: Rows of horror films by the counter in the video store.

'No blue dogs,' I say.

'But I am in love with the blue dog,' she says. 'Don't you remember taking joy in the smallest things?'

'I have learned to group those things together,' I say, 'and take joy in none of them.'

'This is why we have wine connoisseurs and restaurant critics,' she continues, 'film makers and English teachers. This is why we have bird-watchers and moth-catchers, professional sports players and magazine journalists. When people say: Everyone is searching for something, they are talking about the blue dog and all that it could once evoke.'

The little blue dog sits proudly in the middle of the table. I consider snatching it – and throwing it in a river, or melting it. Perhaps it is the way I am glaring at the blue dog – or perhaps, as I suspect, she is so highly strung she can read my thoughts.

'If you ever take the blue dog away from me,' she says, 'I will cry. I won't want to live anymore.'

'You think I'm a monster, don't you?' I say, addressing the question to the blue dog.

Photographs of the Notebook

I used to keep a notebook on my person at all times – to write down ideas, observations, openings for stories. It took me almost a year to realise that the book was hexed, that as long as I had it in my pocket or rucksack I would be blank – not only deaf and blind to the world around me, but mute as well: unable to express even this strange impotence in anything other than silence.

I ripped out all ninety-six pages of the notebook, one by one. I filled the empty leather cover with ninety-six photographs of the notebook and had it rebound. I gave this book of photographs to an artist I know in the city. She sealed it in an envelope and mailed it to herself – so as to copyright the idea – but it must have been lost in the post. She is no longer speaking to me, but that's because of something else.

I shredded the ninety-six ripped-out notebook pages and used them as stuffing in a writing cushion. I took the writing cushion to a shop where it was immediately bought by an old man with pince-nez who has since died in obscurity.

I used so many cameras and films when I was taking the ninety-six photographs of the notebook. Even now a set of photographs will come back to me from the developers and among the smiling friends and rivers and parties, there will be a perfect portrait of the notebook, just there, in between us like a reminder that we're all going to die.

Today I bought a new notebook, but so far this is the only thing I have written in it.

It is not Static

It is not static, but moving forever in decisive circles;
It is not static – and you should listen to those men in Talbot Square
    proclaiming that
It is not static, for they know what they're talking about; see,
It is not static, but sloshing around like waves, or coffee;
It is not static, but shaking like a frightened bear;
It is not static and I hope you read the pamphlet entitled
It Is Not Static the earnest lady handed you last year in which precisely
    how
It is not static is delineated in delightful detail – for instance:
'It is not static, but junting in and out of sleep, stubbornly,' and
'It is not static, but howling into its hands.' It is true:
It is not static – but if you approach the circle of women in long-coats
    and say,
'It is not static, ladies!' they will most probably laugh, declaring,
'It is not static? What idiocy! What rot! It's *nothing* if
It is not static!' and though you are used to such treatment, this will hurt
    you, for
It is not static and of this you are certain, in spite of the Victorian clown,
    howling,
'IT IS NOT STATIC!' sarcastically and honking his nose horn;
It is not static – even though there is no greater power than the power of
    ridicule;
It is not static and lies are often easier to believe; was it not Beloc who
    said of the lie:
'It is not static, but profoundly comfortable'? Perhaps not. If everyone
    realised that
It is not static, maybe something could be done to stop it, but, alas,
It is not static and at this rate it never will be – though don't lose your
    conviction that
It is not static – albeit national newspapers are starting to turn against you.
    Don't give up:
It is not static – although even your girlfriend is beginning to have her
    doubts:

'It is not static? Could it not be just a *little static*?' 'No!' you try to reason
   with her,
'It is NOT static, not in the slightest, not in a million years!' and indeed,
It is not static, but she has that look in her eyes and, as to her allegiance,
   you suspect
It is not static, but pledged to changeable fashions; yet don't let on you
   know
It is not static – she wouldn't like that at all and you need all the help you
   can get, for
It is not static, this bind in which you find yourself, more of a spiral,
   tightening; no,
It is not static. Remember your friend's proposal? 'You must borrow my
   caravan –
It is not static, but can be attached to the back of a car.' It would be nice
   to take a trip:
It is not static, this ennui which afflicts you; but try bawling to *him* that
'It is not static!' and see how long his offer stays open. Poor you:
It is not static – and for this belief you have been made a pariah.

Kit Lambert

The Hitch

A key, turned in the ignition,
Raises in response only weak
Glottal stops. The leaking petrol
Has drawn a perforated line
Out towards the blurred horizon.
He plucks a bag from the back seat,
Puts on shades against midday glare
And stands in the dust by the road,
Thumb jerked skyward, weight on one hip.
The bonnet of his Chevrolet
Yawns open like a crocodile
On the bank of a black river
That flows to human spawning grounds –
Chimney fingers are visible
In smoke flooded valleys below.
After an hour, growing tired,
He sits. After two, his thumb drops.
Four pass & his sandpaper tongue
Pulls him up in search of water,
Only to find his bottle dry.
On the eighth hour, engine growls
Startle him out of wet daydreams
Of waterfalls, lakes, monsoon floods,
But the noise fades, no car appears.
Sixteen, night, he thinks he sees lights
Hover over far off wheat fields,

Unidentified, flying hope.
Twenty four, he sings along to
A radio that doesn't work
And gets angry at advert breaks.
Two days in, circling vultures
Torture him with survival tips
As he plays poker in the sand
Against a pack of hyenas.
Four days, a man on a donkey
Refuses to give him a lift,
'Fred's got a bad back,' the man shrugs,
Fanning himself with a palm leaf.
After a week he notices
For the first time, crickets beat
Wings in time with Beethoven's Fifth
And that blood does taste like chicken.
A fortnight, he writes goodbye notes
To favourite celebrities
But gives up when he can't decide
Between Presley or Costello.
Three weeks, his thirty-first birthday,
A car goes past. It doesn't stop.
Four weeks, devils dance before him,
Angels offer him a bright light.
He shields his eyes, says politely
That perhaps he might start walking.

sonnets from *The Hitch*

II

She was a girl from a snow-painted town
Who sweetened December's milky breath
With chocolate eyes, liquorice hair,
And a sharp, icicle tongue.

We dated in secret
Stealing brief kisses
In stolen cars.

She was a girl from my wind-grated town
With skin like the frozen quarry lake –
I skated over her surface
And waited for her to crack.

She soon grew bored of me.
In a small country,
The nights are long.

V

She grew up with a corn scythe in her hands,
But when her mother taught her how to read
She swapped it for the pages of a book
And harvested knowledge by candlelight.
When marriage was proposed she tried to fight
Against a life as a farmer's whore, cook
And cleaner, but the match had been agreed.
She was married to a blunt, wrinkled man.

After one night she stabbed him in the throat
With the rusted beak of her childhood blade.
As the red stain dried, she went on the run,
Slept in the woods under a sheepskin coat.
The next day she was gone without a trace,
Sun on her back, villanelles on her tongue.

VII.

On sloping fields, werewolves are known to creep
Out of hiding places by moonlight,
To sing until dawn scalds their eyes,
Or men with pitchforks take to the streets.

One evening, a young girl from the village
Sneaks from her bed when the stars blush,
To see what makes the old wives hush
As they sip on cider, play their bridge.

You can still see her, every fourth week
When her fangs are out. She shreds the night
With her song, while her mate pillages
The cattle pens to pay for her touch.

The villagers pretend, tell themselves that she ran,
That she fell in love, left with a nameless man.

VIII

She fell in love, left with a shapeless man who sold bibles (& prophylactics on the sly) to
the carefree glaziers of South Belfast. She had a cruel, angular face, but she was a Lisburn
harpy & her voice could make a man sell his soul for the chance to bury himself in her
flesh. Now this one had buried himself too deeply & the bump was beginning to show.
When winter came & he was reduced to selling cut-priced Gideons down at the local
Travel Inn, she returned to Lisburn to make peace with the family. At first, they cut her

dove into the stew & used her olive branch for firewood. She persevered, bewitched by the lure of central heating & before long the snow covered her tracks.

He stayed in Belfast, waited for her. He trusted that the good book, sold in enough quantity, would see him through. Business was slow. Instincts told him that it was time to move on, that he had reached religious & contraceptive saturation. He started to drink more. He soon became the man (every town has one) that only dogs & children would talk to. They would crowd around him in the churchyard, where he kept a faithful lookout for his Siren. He would drink, tell them strange stories, sing mournful songs.

X

In return for a meal or place to sleep,
There was not much she would not do.
Alone, she worked the inns of barren lands.

One night she met a merchant, a Phoenician
Who asked her to dance for an hour or two
In return for a meal or place to sleep.

He held her close to feel the soft beat
Beneath her cotton dress, asked her to be true
To him, whispered tales of far-off lands.

She told him he could gladly have her hand
In marriage, he asked for the rest of her too.
He took her for a meal, found them a place to sleep.

He saved her from a life upon the streets, but he was a nomad, a restless man.
In return for a meal, a place to sleep, with him she walked the dust of
    many lands.

XII

I wanted to stop, rest, bathe my aching feet. Maher had marched on ahead. It was 25 degrees but still he wore thermal trousers beneath his slacks, his hands thrust deep into his jacket. Everywhere there were building sites, half-built hotels haunted by packs of workmen. They smoked in huddles, threw bits of rubble at a donkey tied to a tree. "Hurry!" Maher shouted. "In winter, the market closes at one. They don't like standing in the cold." I was carrying his bulky, leather case. It looked like the Cypriot who ran the fish stall. Sweat flooded the neckline of my shirt. The walk had made the buka, firewater pushed towards me in a cracked mug the night before, crawl back out of my stomach. The belly dancers, with their drugged snakes & sequin shoes, reappeared. I ran away from them, caught him up.

Passages, the souk's
Labyrinth keeps the sun out,
Keeps the tourists in.

We sleep inside the carpet
Walls of an ancient city.

XIII

Inside the walls of an ancient city,
There is a library deep underground.
Each book is an autobiography
Of a man born out of this land.
When the day comes that they reach seventy
The men are sent into this labyrinth
To write down every memory.
By the light of candles, an army squints
Onto paper the echoes of history,
Arthritic hands scraping at the page.
They are brought food, drink, news of their family,
As they fight against the blurring of age.
When they finish, they are taken to rest in peace.

Each day old men arrive in this city,
To begin to write down their stories.

XIV

They began to write down their story.
&
They began to write-off a storybook
&
They began to writhe with the storyline.
&
They began to wrong-foot their storyteller.
&
They began to xenotransplant a stotty cake.
&
They began to xerox a stowaway.
&
They began to x-ray their straightjackets.
&
They began to yank a stranger.
&
They began to yawn at their stranglehold.
&
They began to yean a strapline.
&
They began to yearn for a strap-on.
&
They began to yell at their strategist.
&
Then they began to yield the stratosphere.

She was a girl from a snow-painted town…

Verona

We woke at seven and by ten fifteen had yawned our way to Verona along the Via Real. It was 1999, but the bus had driven straight from the war. Beth had skipped breakfast and was complaining that her eyes had gone funny, so we stopped at Nico's for pizza. He drank Peroni, peeling off the labels and dropping them on the floor, and we gulped water slower than we could sweat. Maria was pregnant again, gone to McDonalds for her first banana milkshake of the day. We left him at noon watching CNN.

I crossed the road to buy a newspaper, but the man saw me, shouted 'No Sun!'

Scala had summoned us, a cryptic message left in a hotel reception. The street was deserted, the dust turned from yellow to grey, and despite the smell of Soltan I felt cold. We walked slightly apart, as though separated by feuding fathers, as far as Castelvecchio. Suddenly there were tourists everywhere, and others, workers from the cafés and shops, lining the Via Cattaneo and holding photo-negatives up to the light. I looked at Beth, but she just wrinkled her nose and carried on walking. Then a bulging American thrust a sheet of theatrical lighting gel into my hands and grinned encouragingly.

It was at that moment I remembered the date, and a line on a map shown to me by a surfer in Milan that joined Newquay to Bucharest. I gave Beth the sheet, put on my sunglasses, and lifted my face towards the moon.

Ionia

We could only reach Ithaca by boat, too small and hilly for an aircraft to land. It would fall off the end and plunge into the Ionian Sea, coming to rest among triremes and jellyfish. So we came via Cephalonia, and on the way we fished and listened to vowels of a toothless woman, skin like a sun-dried tomato, who saved a space for her husband and told us how the Italians killed him during the war.

'They come to my island, they say they are civilised men. Then they turn into pigs!'

She grinned and whispered to us about her friend who had whispered to the allies about a cave under the harbour, so they could hide their submarines from radar's reach and pop out to take pot shots at passing frigates. The bay was still half a mile away when we jumped into the sea and swam deep underwater, to see whether they were still inside their metal whale, whether nobody had told them the war was over.

Later, we prised sea anemones from rocks, taking these shrunken mines and scooping out the flesh with mussel shells, swearing we liked the taste.

The next month was swallowed as quickly as the watermelon we ate each morning to wash away the ouzo and tar-coffee we drank each night. Maybe it was the smell of salt in a girl's hair as I sat on the back of a moped, or the sound of insects dying, piling up inside our lamp as we played cards for burnt matches on the beach, but I know now why Ulysses came home.

Gift Horse

It was my reward for six months stationed in _
Picking ice from my beard, a chance for glory
And the love of the gods. When I heard the plan
I sacrificed a human liver, amphoras
Littered the ground like battle-strewn corpses.

It was on the morning of _ _ that I was swallowed
Into splintered guts. Through red eyes it looked less horse,
More short-necked giraffe with a mauled cow's head.

I sat in that bovine skull, peered through eye-holes
As they pulled us to the gates, heard the others
Whisper of certain death as they squinted like moles
In the dark, wrote goodbyes to distant lovers.

But those clenched, wooden teeth opened. They dragged us inside, drank,
Tucked themselves into deathbeds. Slept. Gullible _s.

Sarah Law

Fake

You ancient doll. Your wax film of a face
careers across the living room and fills
my vision. I am caught in a breathless womb,
pulse at the plastic yoke your body builds
and am hungry for clouds. I think we sit in rows,
half-hearted as the smoke seeps under doors,
hedging the onus of more leadership. I won't
if you don't first. Misery's twin. My friend.
In shops or in the chapel it's the same:
everywhere an idol doing nothing in the finery
of death. The glass cracks in the dawn and scuppers
defences of pepper spray, rock salt, dew;
and what you feared to love was what you knew.
They offer me a twist of daffodil.

Evolutionary

Look at how I try to talk to you. Spindling
fingers at the collar of your body, eyes
green and gleaming for a meal. Lover, you step
aside and raise the standard. How your faith
is solid and platonic, shielding me. But I'm polluted
into becoming young again, the blue pool
swirls through slits of time and punishes us.
I wish I'd said. I wish I'd said the word.
Thus a combustion, and the slur of tears.
Marbles roll out of my unpacked bag. You sand the plane
and fit the windows in my ball and chain.
Now listen to my attitude of doubt; it liberates
a louche desperation. Gills and gasps proliferate.
I try to surface after it's too late.

Dignified

Noblesse refracted in the scale of grace,
you fighter with an icy mercy. I desire
to join your ranks. I'm grateful for my exile,
tuned to a dance on the moon's crater,
transported in a solitude. Tones signal
your masked arrival, and I turn the corner,
utter the conquered word. Your fabled force
is bliss on my skin, as I slip the noose of thoughts,
float in the air, enact an attitude of trance.
Who's the master after the fact: that foam
slathers the earth as you thirst for home;
and take my snowy back as further proof,
and clutch the pick of fractures from the past,
and chill me like a relic in a glass.

Vegetable

My heart is crushed. My mouth is full of juice.
Machine-pulped, each dumb fruit is concentrate,
each pressure point adds water to the mill, and you're
a cabbage with a mind to kill. Here's a symphony:
gloves twisting the buttons, a suave insanity of manners,
a thug, a knave, a girl. A ring around the wrist is like
a sentence, far from the world's bright hair,
and you tether me to your bad plans, ecstatically.
Out of the arctic comes your carousel, you feed it meat,
and I spit in your eye. The hybrid movement starts
to roar, and all the blades go green, and you imagine
another earth, where language is so much thatch,
dry and combustible under nature's slick;
helpless, deathless, fodder for thunder.

Invisible

Never one to yield to a bleak welcome,
you tell me that this astonishing mist
shrouds a vacancy. I funnel the moist
and empty air into my lungs. A sweetness
settles on our hungry faces. It's wonderful
to sublimate life into a film; your world
a marble; memories like lace. You understand
the study that absorbs the well-wrought man.
I sidle lady-like into this place. The journey,
its planes and saws and fractures, terminates,
and newer lines emerge, loose as hair
flung over skin. Look at us, and shiver, and begin.
I can taste a space for incarnation:
gravity here is a transverse wind.

Psychic

My own good nature eludes me; like a flash
in a fragment of mirror, an old bad thing
I might have done configures and distorts me.
You're a wisp of might-have-been, a thought
I have at night to ease paralysis. At this moment
zealous scribble could have hired me out,
elicited a let-down from a hook, productively
divided what I am. I draw a breath, and wonder
that there are so many left. We prodigy,
brought through intemperance to slavery.
Here I am then, singed at the skull, offering
a vision of the future. Slip a tower into a girl,
and she'll scream, disguise her hair as an old rope,
unravel herself. And close her eyes and hope.

Page

You fetch your book and make me read to you.
I let the brutal images collide
in the mesh of the pain you sketch,
your knife moves quickly over blanks
piercing the skin that separates our mouths.
I'm an uncut parable to you, a strange cry
ripe to spill at a bruise of these dry sheets.

Flare

Night visions of you rustle in my veins,
I dream, alert to every constellation.
I trace your profile onto songs,
twisting in the middle of my bed,
like the heart within your body.
The future leaps and shudders, I start up –
bow and arrow pointing at the sky.
We hunt each other, and I don't ask why.

Silk

Grace comes through your eye,
though I shrink like a sister behind canvas.
Green and white lilies silken my fall;
I know how to knot them, and lie
immune to the news, and twist
myself around, a body fit for sleeping.
I could grow quite easy, imagining
Such a peaceful rending.

Romance

Your text excites me. Sinking in the void,
the warm, the greying screen of dirty water,
you're like a halo on my pearly teeth
minty with that tingle of things hidden.
I love to flirt and you have an abundance
of carry-on filth and the odd tender smile.
Your words build up a net on which I lean,
avoiding the pit where I've lost faith, hope
and the rest of that family of dwarves. I'll
drink to the magic of knowing a distant you.
I break up the trap, step sexily through.
Come home, plummet, crash into the fall.
You are a soft verge, catching me,
Doctor, with your light hand on my brow.

Heritage

The first woman was Selima.
Her fingers were delicate. Four of them tapped
the tanned skin of her arm. The number of children
she would have was as yet undetermined.

The other hand played with a pen – a crude, scratchy
implement. Her thumb pulsed it forward.
Her fingers feathered it back. The lashes
on her closed eyes were innumerable.

Later, she waved the pen as if conducting
birds or the chatter of homecoming men.
She gathered the beats of their swift, irregular notes.
She shaped them into a roundness, a ringing.

I count the Selimas in their rooms, like lights
in cells. She circulates the body, sustaining, pearly.
Write her system down. It decorates, intricate
wedding henna on your unpledged hand,
alight on the moving branches.

Aoife Mannix

How To Be Happy

Eat ice cream, swallow sunshine, cartwheel naked across the moon,
wake early and wrap the dawn around you,
have faith in long, hot baths by candlelight,
never wear high heels, only drink to remember,
make mornings in bed a special occasion,
buy flowers for yourself, celebrate chocolate,
break mirrors, throw pint glasses into rivers,
have sex in public places and erotic fantasies on buses,
avoid the underground, give up traffic jams,
don't walk when you can fly,
be as old as supernovas and as young as snow,
talk to animals, die your hair, wear sunglasses,
eat croissants for breakfast, stay up past your bedtime,
meet the love of your life on a long stroll home after midnight,
snog total strangers, never check your change,
don't set your watch to the local time,
collect aeroplanes, ban paperwork,
declare war on your bank manager, local council
    or other large faceless bureaucracy
that can be the focus of your aggression,
don't fill in questionnaires, tick boxes, accept labels,
never check the price of something you already bought, believe in bargains,
regret what you do, not what you don't,
learn to cook, learn to apologise, how to complete visa applications,
travel so that you know what it is to come home,
don't underestimate people, collect kisses, buttons, and birthday cards,
say what you mean, ignore the expectations of others,
dance in your kitchen, listen to CDs by bands you never heard of,
pop bubbles, chew gum and keep singing even if you're out of tune,
do things that aren't in character, the only person worth shocking is yourself,

wear socks that don't match, don't tie your laces
   when you're told they're undone,
never make a phone call hoping to get an answering machine,
ring people back, skip guilt, long queues and raw meat,
read sell by dates, accept endings, understand goodbyes,
don't let go of a good thing,
allow the curve of a neck, the flash of a smile to shatter your world,
be turned on by winks,
don't believe in answers, ignore television,
lose yourself in sentimental films, watch Casablanca every Christmas,
don't be afraid of subtitles, shuffle words, play the lottery,
ask your lover for a tissue, forget to be embarrassed,
get on your knees and beg them not to leave you,
   but practice the art of packing suitcases,
go skinny dipping, lose your shadow, drop down a rabbit hole,
don't keep your friends waiting, but grow up in your own time,
stop trying to prove something, wear clothes that fit,
never diet, lie about your age or shag someone you don't fancy,
fall in love as often as you can, but don't stay unrequited,
tell the truth whenever possible,
make your own fashion statements, but don't take them seriously,
suspend your disbelief, critical judgment,
   give romance the benefit of the doubt,
be a fool but not a martyr,
experiment with kleptomania, burning down houses, and other drugs,
but don't make it the sole subject of your conversation,
try not to bore people, admit when you're wrong,
have faith in angels but not in God,
see ghosts, get kidnapped by aliens,
tell silly jokes, die laughing,
and most of all forgive yourself,
dare to be devastated,
open your eyes and see all that you could lose,
protect your sense of adventure,
and never take advice.

Ache

a cubic space of oxygen,
just as I'm turning back,
you're there like a secret I never knew,
like everything falling from a great height,
having drinks in strange bars where you speak French
when you're angry,
and I understand just how unbearably light you are
like I want to go home with you,
but you wink at the bus stop,
just a bass line shiver down my spine
as I head off into a night
that is suddenly burning so hard and so true
like my skin is in flames
and if I don't touch you now
I'll stop breathing all together.
So little time in my fear, my excuses,
all the places I'm meant to be,
this is just a temporary snowball gathering speed,
splitting me into a thousand fragments
of being this stranger that loves the music in your eyes,
the basic fact of your skin on mine,
so simple and sheltered,
this is some kind of homecoming,
but I tear the phone calls in two
and I'm so afraid of how much I want you,
it's not normal, it's not me,
I could say it out loud, but if the words escape from me,
how can I ever put them back?

Come Back

I'm stuck in fluorescent hell and as I'm inching up the queue,
I feel so exhausted, like all the joy has been sucked
　　from the marrow of my bones,
and I want so badly to go home.
When you won't meet my eye, I push you to the stairway
and you say I banged your head so hard, you didn't know where you were.
Black Goth guitar smoke as I stood staring at you,
and wanting you more than I could breathe.
I wish I could kiss you in public,
hold you so fast and so tight.
No one can tell me this is wrong,
this is not the path to take.
This is where I've come back to,
your eyes as round as whole mornings in bed,
and the moving men drumming through the wall.
They're getting closer, but I'll protect you,
I'll keep you in the palm of my hand.
And no one smells as good as you.
The music in your bedroom fills concert halls,
and if I can be with you, then all the crazy mad space
　　of never knowing where I am
can explode into some kiss that falls over and over
as in a dream where I no longer have to wonder where I'm going to land.
We could sail off the edge of the earth and they'll never catch us.
You spring your wings from secret places.

But that's unfair to water as you flow through my hands,
and this morning when the alarm cracks open your suitcase,
is it always going to be like this?
Little snips of kisses, and as you kiss my lips, sure and slow,
I wonder if I grabbed you and begged you to stay,
would that make me ridiculous?
When our lives are divided in pieces, shooting back and forth
　　under the ocean.

Your hair as I press my face into it, just the echo of your smile,
makes me want to hug myself,
like the streets are empty when you're not around,
and it always seems to rain, it never used to rain like this.
You'll phone when you get there, but I can't eat telephone calls,
and the flat is as empty and dull as the grey sky.
I open the curtains to watch your back retreating and think,
come back, come back and stay.
Can't there be somewhere for us
so that we're not stripping our Sundays of leaves,
and I'm not sure if I can go on saying goodbye like this,
it's just a whisper of where I should be,
   trying to pretend this performance is me.

What We Used To Listen To

It's exactly the same record my mother had years ago.
Funny how music collapses time and space.
I'm back lying on the cream sofa with the blue lines like veins.
She turns the volume up, telling me tales of Switzerland,
an ex boyfriend who tried to run her over with his car.
And if she'd married him, I'd be one of those Swiss chocolate girls
with blond plaits curled around their heads.
I can't imagine this and laughing, she takes my hands,
swirls me round the glass table. The beat of love escaped.
How my father asked her to dance, and all time crumbled to the ground.
In that song in which I began, all stories meet in the end.
My mother denying her sudden tears, her youth swaying through the door.
I didn't understand then how her smile could be so sad,
how music plays such cruel tricks on the heart.

Prophet

The man with the birds in his eyes went walking,
and he drank the sky till the sea was a desert.
His feet ached with the rhythm of his magic.
He unfolded himself by the water,
spreading his black skin, a blanket with stars,
tiny pin pricks of illumination.
Islands with lighthouses,
a lamp swaying back and forth,
a white shirt waving in the wind.
Dreams rinsed and wrung dry.
The water burns with words
and the trees whistle round the houses.
In the deep bass of his voice,
there are wings that melt,
clapping hands
rising above and beyond what we know ourselves to be.
This song is a mystery, this life is a test,
and some souls are older then others.
When Armageddon catches up with me,
this is the music I will carry in my bones.
The heart break of a mythical nation,
God humming in my ear.
This silence is not empty
and this earth is the dust of millions.
History is whispering.
If you listen, you will hear.
This water holds memory,
this connection is healing.

Songs I Used To Know

A small orange radio,
a birthday present from my best friend
when I was nine years old.
My favourite part the ear phones,
hiding under the covers
in the dark cave of my imagined bomb shelter,
I plugged them deep into my ears,
spun the dial, the crackle of half dreams,
I found those songs for myself.
The whispered voices of old men
splitting their hearts open,
all that homesickness washing over me,
the ache of their loneliness,
the battles they fought,
and I couldn't understand then how love was lost.
The way they traveled too far to come back,
the beating of the drums, the echo of gunfire,
the boats leaving at dawn,
a bow drawn across a string,
a country abandoned.
The drink and the poverty
and the sheer wildness of their words stripped to the bone.
In school they lined up history,
the dates scratched on the blackboard,
but it never cut me
the way those melodies seeped into my fingers,
the tapping on a table,
and much later when I boarded the aeroplane,
throwing myself into the big city,
like a tune I couldn't quite catch,
I wandered the streets of emptiness,
trying to find those old beats,
suddenly their rhythm in my feet.

Sometimes to become a stranger
is to find our own music everywhere.

Harder Coming Back

I packed in a swirling rush of love, airports,
making my fortune,
high on adventure, city smells,
the endless streets of being young and foolish,
not counting how much time I had in my pocket.
London drank me up,
before I knew where I was on a rainy afternoon,
I lay exhausted on concrete,
trying to figure out how to swim back.
But the faces turned into strangers,
the old flats are being knocked down,
their windows empty sockets
and the kids playing football have moved on.
The local pub still there
but stepping in like a tardis,
three times as big, all metal and shining.
I sit in the corner, a shadow of myself,
and only then does it hit me.
Hundreds of years have passed,
the place I left has sunk to the bottom of the ocean.
I am Oisin, I am Atlantis,
an endangered species, a space traveler with no compass.
The words of that old song beat in my ears,
'it's a long, long way, it gets further every day',
and I am a foreigner in my own home.

Sophie Mayer

Skating to Antarctica

'for a time there, I thought we had lost the desert'

We began a little north, in blue Holland, and
travelled south fleeting

over frozen canals. It's a fairy tale (one worth the
telling); a legend we subscribe to like a watchman's fire.

The south grew heady and moved among us, dark
with aspirations,

with evening tea. The smoke-red altar of
Morocco smelt of something not quite saffron –

but heat went with us, packed in shoes like sand. Cambridge
was just a breath

on a grey-cold double-glazed window pane, just
solemn, wandering, unremembered dreams,

just a longing for sands. To continue: down
around the world

chill encroaching, we leapt (designedly)
across the scorch of Africa and stepped

on ice. Destination. The warm spaces
of life narrow-

ing. A shaft of memory: coals spitting
against fragrant pine and flesh. Bracing

cold. Embracing. We cannot skate here hand
in hand, the ice –

not smooth like sand that slips and gives
a sense of soft infinity – a solid mass

of time, a foundering beneath footsteps.
A particular

vision. A myth. A stride.
A sliver embedded in our one true eye, and sparkling.

Cambridge Sonata

'I went into the secret rooms
and lounged and lay on their beds.

I went into the secret rooms
considered shameful even to name.
But not shameful to me – because if they were,
what kind of poet, what kind of artist would I be?

> C.P. Cavafy, 'And I lounged and lay on their beds,' September 1915
> translated by Edmund Keeley and Phillip Sherrard

Constantin, I have caught your September mood
sitting in this cold Alexandria. (How I wish it would burn).

Amidst the offered knowledge, I seek the questions
that you mouthed to the ceiling fan at an Egyptian

summer's end as the boys donned kefiya in the evening
cool. Your greekfrenchenglish tongue lolling,

syllables saliva-hot. Where is Alexandria? Burnt city,
burnt again. Your death, a memory of burning

keeps me warm as autumn becomes autumn here.
The heating hums (invisible) like a ceiling fan

in this most commonplace of rooms, inhabited
as bedroom, living room, room of decisions and

laughter. Universal synthesis of comfort and
boredom, of kettles and off-white tones against

polished wood. Oxymoron: an empty college,
collection of nothing but the rain we walk in

and slip on. The smell of. Where is Alexandria
when I need it? Your poems next to the *Seven Pillars*

of Wisdom on my shelf, next to Catullus –
definition of boy-spine against spine, warm vertebrae

of letters telling me you speak of the rooms I
cannot find. And if I did I would lose the keys

and find myself on your doorstep, burning
with a desire that does not exist. No decorum.

No books, no stories written about this rush
that says *Your poems become me like autumn*

becoming autumn. I watch the leaves
and they are like dancing to Fred Astaire. A desire does not

exist while dancing that is not fulfilled. Ephemera
of footsteps. How can they leave no mark

on the carpet? Off-white. My hands are small and cold
like leaves. I have seen him before, my

dancer. I have seen him in the secret room and
pressed my nose to the glass steamy with coal-

heat and the sweat of a single body that can be
neither touched nor loved nor ignored

with impunity. Constantin, the bed in the room
I seek is smooth as experienced skin, wide as

a photograph of mountains I have never seen.
Perhaps as white as snow that melts and I remember

the delicious sensation of cold air, cold water,
stepping from the wet swelter. The clear cold of

glass against my body as I watch him move
into the secret room. What kind of poet am I –

not to follow him. To follow him with arms
of envy, glass of amber tea in hand saying

We will have our afternoon of ceiling fans,
our sweat the only part of us that is

touching. We have had our morning of
the naked glance, the cast of eyes, dis-

interested. Perhaps I am an ascetic by virtue
of my tiny hands that could not bunch the

sheets of experience. So much for virtue.
I would like to be in keeping with my poetry,

with your poetry, I would like to keep it close
to what is kept in the crevices and blankness

of my memory. It has no front rooms, the house
of pleasure behind my eyes. The steps lead down

from the attic and end in my mouth. So all secrets
are out. The secret room is on my tongue

and open to all. I tell you this, Constantin,
because you could have been him and

I could have been you. It's a commonplace,
a bed too neat to lounge on, a scrounged

phrase that I will not return or relinquish.
You did not return to their beds.

Blue Love

So certain that I will burn some days
like leaves
which redden in the autumn cold.

Days are clear, effervescent with clouds,
sunlight, galleries
where we meet and you teach me things.

Listen: *white light is divisible*
by glass
and other refractory media.

Liquefying, somehow, to find
blue amidst
the clarity of all that clarity

possesses. It is like music you
say, but
never explain what music is like.

I glimmer through the speaker of the phone
and know
that Bach is turquoise, Rameau indigo sometimes,

Mozart a smash of cyan. But I am blue, also, un-
musical. Melody
estranges me from you, even when,

listening, I hear you sometimes in the mass
and volume
of the notes. Blueness comes

from the face of the speakers. So this is
light. So
this is what we mean by *light*

when we say love, prismatic. Dancing. *Spect–*
meaning *seen.*
But unfinished. And if I see the melody, that

is listening. (I'm learning). And if that is
listening, then
what is there left to learn but love?

Self-Portrait as αthene

I see myself as sculpture some
days, lost as marble
on a hillside.

He is in Athens in pieces. A blood-red poppy.

α

On the white-painted wall
of a house where
I never lived is
a photo of
him.

I could pull that ponytail out of the frame and say

α

pale arms
ox eyes
breast
plate

yes, I have always liked the word attribute

α

Hey! Pretty boy hey!
mummy's boy.
Boy, hey
can we hang

for a while on this angry beach?

α

I promise to
laugh and
be

immortal.

α

I see the double shadows the firelight makes on the walls of your tent

α

Too old for you, trouble,
you'll kill yourself
over him

because he would over you. And I

α

muscular golden river flowing death's-red
one crocus-word, one burning.
The horses' fear is mine. I
see you rise and fall, a
sword washed
clean

by the wine-bright stream.

α

you are golden
boy in fire-
light your

eyes tearlit

α
I told
you
so

well, fate showed me alright

α
hillside scattered
with bodies like
fragments

of a sculpture. Of me.

Fauré's Requiem

I confess: I have let my mind wander
into yours. This should be forbidden, here
amidst the incense and choirboys
whose faces so resemble yours. I'd pay
to see you surpliced white and singing. I'd
place my cheek against these railings, and hide
the clouds that rise like Gloria. My heart is
strange here, unchristian. Damn eternal bliss.
I want it now. Voices, vaulting, promise
the life to come. I won't be saved. I try
to counter constant thoughts of earthly joy,
but Fauré and my faded heartbeat blur.
Unrequited love's a Christian calling;
to attain salvation in the grace of falling.

Joanne Merriam

Auto Biographies

I remember my breath making tiny clouds. My hands mittened on the wheel. The crescent moon high up in the clear sky. I remember the mudflats to the horizon, your laugh and your hand on my thigh. I remember fog waiting doglike at the foot of the mountain. A doe we slowed down for, her eyes redefining silver in the high beams. The open window turning your hair into a bird.

I remember you breaking the dashboard with your fists. My stillness. A hawk on a birch branch. The way the plastic pops back into place. I remember the black ice slide into the median and the twisted axle. A few spooky bits where trees rose up out of flooded, frozen fields. A few grains of snow piled up in corners. Road kill.

I remember saying I loved you, and later saying I didn't anymore. I remember the way the snow skating over the pavement made shapes that faded as we named them. I remember crying. I remember you crying. Our voices, fences in the darkness, and the riverbeds lined with a mess of broken ice.

The Kiss

As she talks, their foreheads touch.
The garden is all around them.
The rasp of water in the fountain makes the night
more impenetrable. He reaches out

to move strands of her hair back behind her ear.
The water caresses the emerald
crazy spring, in love
with the new velvet whorl of her petal lips,
and they fall into each other,

and the sky opens
and a mantle of tempests comes,
ending the silence in the groves.
Overcome by water,
their petals fall on their knees,
their innocent movements,

the frisky roses all nude and dizzy.

Mirror Points

Somewhere patio lanterns swing softly through fog and the smell of salt. Somewhere your cat, ginger-haired, precise in the placement of its feet, sitting on the ledge created by the open double windows, watches through the screen the leaves of the red maple drip rain on one another. Somewhere particles, to the north and to the south, spiral around a geomagnetic field line.

Somewhere the lingering juice of strawberries brings your tongue to your lips. Trapped between two mirror points, I already hear them yielding, the rasp of your teeth over those tiny seeds, as the others reach for your fingertips from the bowl. Red stains feather across your wet fingers, a pattern like the veins of leaves. Somewhere an ion or electron slows as it enters a stronger magnetic field, and is turned back. Somewhere your hand tightens on a waist and your fingers pinch almost to pain.

The overhead fan turns lazily, barely stirring the air, which is not only still but still warm, and steam from the shower fills the room as your fingers loosen with heat. Somewhere the stronger field makes the spiral flatten and unwind in the opposite direction. I can feel your skin even miles away, a tactile memory real as salt, as soap, as ashes.

And somewhere a vocal line opens on a fluttering note – fragile as shale, frenetic as plovers – and suddenly the magnetosphere becomes you. Everything is made of sunlight and wings, cyclotron motion, iridescent feathers, helical trajectories, jewel tones, and we glance off them like a stone off a pond.

Old Sailors Become Seagulls

for my grandfather

1

On its head the sky perches
velvet with morning clouds. Scissoring
its wings in that lurching
taking off
the seagull shifts
its gray weight from wire to air

ready with a tale about the navy,
shipbuilding days, my father as a child.
Soul-birds, I remember
from one story of sailors and reincarnation,
scavengers you fed through a wild summer
against all common sense
because of your father and his brothers,
lost at sea.

2

Your breath leaves your chest
and pivots in a distant v,
salt air embedded in your scrawny
bird body,

you've escaped from the necessity of speech,
from gravity, the cancer ward
and its blue light, escaped

into this telephone wire sanctuary,
sewer outlet luxury feast.

Throwing Signs

When I was mean I was the rolled-up newspaper, the bent coat hanger, the torch. I was the unknown footprint drying on the porch. I was absinthe disguised as lime. I was state-sponsored bindweed whitening a ditch. When I was mean I was a bitch who told strangers I loved only them and meant it every time.

When I was six I loved to burn ants with a magnifying glass. I turned beetles on their backs to watch them dance. At sixteen did the same to men. I was the fan that barely stirs the heat and I was baby's breath hanging to dry. I was the bite of cayenne. I was the sky.

When I was mean there was no room for the rest of me. There was no rest for me. I was in the details: I was the crisp line of your teeth traced in the apple's skin; the string dangling off the broken violin; the sweat on the soldier's forehead and the hand that shoots; the hurricane pulling up the graveyard trees and with them the coffins resting on their roots; the saliva in your cup. After every fight I was your reason to keep getting up.

What Sharp Teeth You Have

1

At age 16 she installed a droll concubine in the gallery of her eyes, took to corduroy hip huggers and cigarettes.

Her name-day gifts smouldered under that sun; sharp summer shrieks under the garden hose graduated to his car seat.

2

When I remember my dreams they're time-lapse photography, a landscape like our bodies intertwined. The barren hills your surgeon knuckles, the contours of your face the clouds at storm; my fingers the scenery in your words.

Your lips map mine, annex my breath.

3

Their husbands are these bobbing plastic animals boxed in by inner tubes and paddle boards, lips fused apart in a white grin, while the wives patrol the tiles in pairs, saying, 'I can't believe he forgot.

Again.' Behind their voices hides the sharp hiss of air escaping. Their bathing suits stay dry. The husbands clutch at their big bellies as the bubbles break around them.

4

The wolf at the door doesn't know jack about domesticity. Gonna blow your house down but who's afraid? When he struggles into his pants at 3 am you're never surprised.

You know enough about wolves to know the time he's wasted you won't get back.

The King's Ransom

I get the concept from an online discussion, a stranger talking about the perfect day: 18 holes of golf, a certain kind of cigar and a shot of a certain drink, a massage and a blowjob. Others list a wild gig where the bar's jumping, strawberries and wine, swimming off a Sicilian beach, a puppy, total silence for three hours.

Mine's that July day we went to Peggy's Cove, the sky was mostly clear and the water hit the rocks with more than the usual force. The spray was dramatic. You had lobster for the first time. The car took the curves with more than the usual aplomb and on the way home the cell rang, my sister had given birth, an apgar-perfect girl. My distracted mother said, "You're a niece!" and we all laughed.

God Bless This Twenty Dollar Bill

Silence glares back at you from hubcaps, from the bus' wheels, from the graffiti on the brick. The songbirds sound sick. You can't make the rent and there's no more booze. Don't turn on the stove. You'll blow the fuse. You check every payphone for change.

You're out of bridge tokens. The left back burner's broken and mildew stains the windowsill. God bless this twenty dollar bill. The cracks in the bathroom mirror make real look strange. The city presses its ear to the open, breathing triangle of your window frame's warp –

your voice in the shower a delicious pulse in your throat
backlit by the echo against the tile,
every drop percussive, the way
the water drips off your hair and

love waits for you

with his face wrinkled by the weight of itself
against feathers,
muttering in his sleep in the too-small bed with the broken springs,
but disrepair doesn't matter now,
because the sun swallows you casually,
because there's sufficient, just for this morning, and because
he'll be awake any moment.
Just think how time alters everything, especially
this –

and you can't bring yourself to care about the crack in the bathroom plaster stretching taller still. Oh, God must have blessed this twenty dollar bill.

Snorkeling

We stayed up all night talking
of galleons full of bones and gold,
imagined light falling where logic denied it.

Faces down, we kept an eye out
for brightly darting anythings;
your hands that dipped into mine

now puddle under linen and wood paneling.
The water's not clear anymore.
You've surfaced – fins dangling by your sides –

when I imagine you it's as you were then,
heavy with weightlessness, drenched
in impossible light.

George Messo

The Beautiful Apartments

'The thought working its way towards the light.'
   – Ludwig Wittgenstein, 1946

In the empty block
across the lake from here
you notice first a light
go on go off go on again.

You wonder who
at this late hour
stirs in rooms
darkness uninhabits.

And then yourself, alone,
gazing from a room
towards the light
across the lake from here.

Sleepwalking / Medical Notes

Doors snap in the wind.
Three days ill,
and it is snowing.

Ungaretti said it first:
The pointlessness of solitude.
Yashar, whose name means life,

you are three years dead
and I am still in the State Hospital, Ankara.

They think I'm lunatic, call me somnambulist,
say I ate the sun and became darkness.

•

Doors snap in the wind, doors
you could leave my room to close,
wake me from the recent past,
as if from a light sleep.

Faces crowd the portal:
snow in their hair, breath frosting the glass.

Entrances
for Michael Lowenthal

All morning climbing down the wooded gorge
who knows sometimes the loneliness you move towards
or where you unexpectedly are lost in mud and greenage
finally to be among the river's thickest coils

in silence oh my God and nothing there but beauty
not enough the silvering of water-quiffs or fish
which rise imperceptibly to flies or what
you think may even be seed-pods floating by.

Bored, as you are, with constant re-description
no longer swayed by frightful sounds –
named inner lives, imagined selves
– you opt to leave the afternoon
and step, one naked foot, into the Choruh river.

Unmistakably it is light
fading or else failing always
into which you will emerge –

the wish to be there, suddenly real,
puts everything in its place.

Visiting the Greek House of Yashar Chalik, with Musa Kul *

I

We come we do
not know for the last time,

a city's edge fenced out,
a pavement's terminal gate.

This is where you made a home
and where the home made you.

The garden is a lapis-work
of leaf and branch and stem.

II

What's overlooked, or left behind
when a house walks out on life?

A kind of grief, its slow increase
and contradictory urge

to speak, and hold its tongue.
We will not say you're dying now,

so neither of us know.
The husked vowels you chase

are your own voice, calling out
"Kübraa! Kübraa!"

Where does she go
this girl of yours

lost among the hazel grove
when there you sleep in grass

and wake to a different word?
Your hair unkempt,

but still it is your hair
and the garden ours for now.

*Commissioned by the Turkish Magazine *Kül* as part of an exhibition '40
Photographs, 40 Writers' and first shown, in Turkish, on the Ankara Underground.

Fruit Music

The cherry tree
and its body-buds
quote pleasure.

Quote 'body'
and it buds
the cherry pleasure.

The pleasure tree
buds and quotes
'cherry
        cherry
                cherry.'

from *Notes from the Haft Awrang*

1. *The Wise Old Man*

Not what they are but what they seem,
Scenes from the far side of a dream.

The wise old man chides a foolish youth.
Staring through the boy the old man finds

The hare behind a rise half its size
Gazing at the rock-toned mountain fox.

The fox looks skyward, finds the bear
Fixing on the deer. The deer in turn

Finds perching doves below a racing cloud.
The formulas are the same, after all

What are birds without a tree in which
To be themselves the mirror of human

Company? There is for once no human-
Headed horse to say what must be said.

While the old man chides a foolish youth
Wisdom, instead, speaks with a bird's mouth.

Two Siberias

1. An Essay

This essay is the story of two Chekovs. The she of it after a while deports to a distant place. Let's call it Siberia. One day, today, the he of it is alone, again. The story does not go well. So much did, in her life, happen. Truth was a mystery and therefore useless, the gangrenous toes themselves an unwanted fact. In the end the woman who is, however, a bourgeois eats only holes, becomes whole.

2. A Turk in the Hotel Gulag

In Moscow, morbid, sick for home
You claw the breast of exile.
Siberia is far away,
The night wood mute with snow.

But this is not your shame
To fear death and dream it.
You never lost your faith for long.
You got off the train, Brodsky stepped on.

Siberia is far away,
The night wood mute with snow.

Fragments of a Black Sea Mountain Poem

His pocketbook. We read of 'smallness overlooked', of gathering mass, 'no greater than a stone, before an edge it's falling from.' And would I look, asks Dr Kul, the matter of another's mind, me being of the mountain going kind? In here, I say, we do not always speak the things we mean to say. He was, for one, thinking 'çig' when mistranslating 'avalanche.' In point of fact and from the fragments here dislodged we see him meaning 'landslide', 'rockfall', 'wave of stone'.

What hope in all of this? asks Dr Kul. We notice only smallnesses, as if the hill intrudes. But what is this? 'O merciful God, everything is almost too much itself. Here we go again with our small hands. The mountain does not know us, but still we tug at its sleeve.'

I Close My Eyes

There are simpler things returning to us. Close your eyes. Whoever it is we
think we are across this landscape making us, a different voice is speaking to
you now. You're on the coastal road. The blue of yet another sky is veining
through its cloud. Your clothes, electric wet, are charged against your skin.
We're toeing the lip of a hole we'll spend a lifetime falling through. I close
my eyes, and only then the sound restates the place: heavy tread of bodies
down from hill farms loaded up with roots; wet-releasing earth-oils; herb-rich
voices; Black Sea gulls. And who are they to think our knowing them makes
a difference to the world or way our seeing eyes turn in upon themselves.

There are simpler things returning now. Close your eyes. Whoever it is we
think we are across this space where language makes us foreign to ourselves…
I close my eyes. You're on the coastal road. I have taken from its found abode
your heart and place it here with me.

Anouk Mishti

No Pretence

'How bizarre to go back in time, six maybe
in England; sherbert and comics in bed
playing with white kids, watching Zebedee,
Playaway, Pugwash with little ditties to note,
though no pretence to hear what they said;
but eight was Christmas in the hot desert
with pop-corn, Jackson Five and Navajos,
the first time for us to taste the white snows
after which came more England, 007
jolly hockeysticks and posh St. Trinian
school which the original 'grey bomber'
gals were inspired by; from here to your
world where imperial feathers had to accept the view –
with stark wooden smells and books
reflecting your history, but not to embellish
it with fact or friction, say, about World War Two
(Indians and Ceylonese fried side by side)
but were hushed for no reason than it takes
some places longer to know when they've lost
the Koh-i-noor and its 'smiling lakes'
despite how often they are told;
it appears to be turning at the heart,
Vikram Seth is one, Roy also knows the cost
of eloquence and Hinglish spoken wide,
whichever way you want to see the host
it has 'a better karma' to be in a distant part
in one sense, as long as you are able to toast
the swelling forces of the dark
countries which rise against a coast.'

I Look

I look on W.W.W. PERINPANAYAGAM and find
my given name three times,
now three uncles and an aunty
and still famous a VIP,
my 1890 paternal grandfather;
then my parents and my brother's
and two hundred more of the antique hierarchy,
you know it's a native joke
as we're all related somehow
hailing from 'Little England',
an island race now
scattered in the circular
matter of isolation
and I don't know half of them
as I search through – many cut dead,
caught in the cross-fires of integrity
demanding to be recognised
with the grandfather on the internet,
the Christianised and faithful gent
baptized as an Englishman
who Tamilised his name right back again,
while the habitual jokes wore thin,
they may be called back to some 21st century tiger-torn idiom.

Saraband

Gabriela, your voice throws a line to me,
pulling me in through your latticed door.
Your piercing grace invites me in, to see

your Spanish print of a Chilean blood-tree.
It says 'look here, read on, hear more'
from *Sonetos de Muerte*, your almond legato.

Slow Rain of nature's earth; you tempt me
in, the honourary dame swaying
upon your fêted grace. Your velvet drops stop me dead.

The Saraband guidance lays ahead, to be
met by *Sor Juana*, unbound poet-nun before
replying to Sor Filotea de la Cruz. Recall her desire –

I hear *My Mother*. I spin lean black letters
to lie still.
Your tinted grace pricks my doubts. I drink to

Lucila Godoy Alacayaga, a crafted blade of theatre
who can turn my grey head black once more.
Dancing in ageless urgency,
I start to sing, to sway, to fall – step up, to see.

Jet

The hero himself was made in Surinam,
gallant in tincturely affection, trading
fish and marmosets, marvellously shaped skins
Parakeetoes, Macaws and little rarities dripping
the dress of an Indian Queen; seeing
flies as big as fists as art cannot imitate,
baskets of axes, needles and knives,
shining trinkets in ears, lips and merchandise sold
beats Adam and Eve prettily woven
in coloured feathers, in new oiling
hides of brick, but soft and sleek
like our 'parents' before the Fall.
Handsome young Indian dying of love
for a beautiful young Indian maid,
Imoinda of honour; not yet to be slaves
they cast off the war captains and their plural wives
who all have the boon of *cousheries*.
One son left, the rest dead, the young man entered the field of Mars.
Folding arms, eyes and sighs, courting
the first state of innocence,
shooting oranges and other fruit
in the virtuous wood and savannas
seeking eatable beasts, behooving them to
split hairs with arrows with masters of freight,
the blacks show novelty, not heightened curiosity
and their native justice knows no fraud.
The dying king of Coramantien
accepted the wisdom of Oroonoko Moor
Spanish, French and English speaker
set off in piercing white eyes and teeth of snow;
illustrious courtier of Christendom, teak-high
pretty tall, exacting handsomely
his face of perfect ebony and polished jet,

hair turned down by the aid of arts
topped by Caeser's nose, raising
the patterns of incensing beauty,
only fitting that he finished trading
his life and his constant bride's, falling upon
the imperial taste of mangled kings.

Ring

I wondered about the history of this ring
being so prominent, almost appearing in the flesh.
Do you remember him saying 'Ducats! Ducats!'
His gentle daughter, traded with too much gold,
caught up together because of the tribal laws,
but the prosecution believed something else. It started with food,

I think. It's the same for Muslims. Food
means no pork. Even the napkin rings
in his house were controlled to keep the laws
of strictures. Did he really drive his flesh
and blood away like that? I couldn't do it over my gold
jewels however precious the caskets of bullion ducats.

Rupees, lire, cents, dollars, pounds, dinars, ducats
– it's all in bonds but we should be breaking food
together. He refused dinner in the end, like my silver and gold.
His servant hates him almost to death; he runs rings
around him. If I could get a pound of flesh
for every time that pauper breaks the household laws,

I'd be rich by now. For the master, the laws
meant there was no dice with ducats
or bribes of silver or slaves three times over but his flesh
was as human as mine. You ask about the food,
but what about his wife's wedding ring
that his daughter lost? Nothing replaces that kind of gold.

We now know that the nuptial metal was brick gold,
hard like platinum. The judge kept testing the laws
of the land, eradicating the subject of the ring,
and amusing himself in court. 'Duck it! Duck it!'
he shouted jovially, the near-death sentence being passed off in foody
crudities, and he won. He didn't allow the pound of flesh

to materialise. The flesh and meat of ancient laws
sat on the man, lost daughter, ducats and her mother's gold
ring, for chasing the pink-pork itch of fast food.

It

One day, the passionate Gangadis
could not contain himself, so aimed
to surprise Koonis, the innocent young maid
who said 'yes', not worrying to defend herself.
And with each touch her desire was aroused.
With his burning, trembling hands he pressed
on her swelling, heaving, fretting breasts
while he spent himself already, panting in his lust.
She, bitten with eager fire, matching the basest instinct,
cried "I want you more!". Performing the sacrifice

the potent God was invoked, as poets still pretend
to do, helping to take her 'innocence' once more,
but slower. The too transported hapless pawn
finds the colossal pleasure had turned him tame.
Koonis tried to lend a hand for one last chance;
still soft with desire, she caressed his torso
and slipped her gentle hand down to reawaken
the dead cinder – momentarily, willing it to dance
Up. But it obeyed itself, the rubbery Priapus
staying awhile, while her lips searched his wanting face.

All her unguarded beauties omitted away, thrown
in the instant for the pursuit of her flaming requires
still leaves his lethargic prick in its whore-tired
refusal to be aroused. As it belittles itself, it finds
its slippery cover, a snake in the grass, so cold
like the decaying flower soaked in the dawning dew.
Sulking feverishly, he puked and mewled
'It's all your fault Koonis, and you didn't even bleed!'
She said nothing, instead rolling over in her drying thirst
musing over the resilience of common or garden fucking posts.

Sensuous Moves

means
starting with your tongue-tip;
  Watch you don't scare her
  by biting too hard. Like this.
Touch her lightly
with tender strokes,
  and careful to
  hold back your weight of lust.
Caress her breasts
with your most artistic touch.
  Don't rush her
  by squeezing too tight. Like this.
Make love as I instruct you -
best unhurried
  Don't press yourself on her
  by being salaciously quick.

~~~~~~~~~~~~~~~~~~~~~~~~~~~~~~~~~

I don't know if you
in truth, appreciate what
I'm doing, young Prince.
You need practice to be accomplished.
You will never master singing or
reciting poetry like us.
When you make love to her and
lose yourself in desire,
will you remember our
rehearsal, my young buck?

~~~~~~~~~~~~~~~~~~~~~~~~~~~~~~~

If I ask her just to hold on,
        she moves more closely
        towards my lips, to pleasure-peck them.

If I ask her to slow down,
        she undoes her sari blouse – her nipples ripe,
        and unwraps herself. Leisurely…but
if I ask her to let me have my say
because she is being too audacious
        she curses me wildly.

If I tell her of promises not
to have a woman in my bed,
        she leaps onto it
        to taunt me.

Unhesitatingly, unresistingly
I savour the fruit of her openness.
She embraces me with her butterfly whispers
of love, to devour me once and too much again

        How can I keep away?
If I ask myself, I want only to stay.

She Wore the Piano Keys

She wore the piano keys with restraint, to activate
breakfast in the cherry; there was a pleasure in having
earrings on toast any time of the day, watching
the orchestra dining in puddles; the essence of
hush puppies purring by, painted with diamond croutons.

She always cleaned her eyes with vanilla topping
while sewing the cricket on jazz radio, but
the fingernail broke down with three passengers, and
at the same time, the prime minister swallowed the ladder.

The voice tapped him on the shoulder, and
the pincushion chose his tie and cuffs carefully;
the lift spoke eloquently at the fence ball, guests
from across the sea, urchins, and the balloons
ran amok in the aubergine tunnels and swimming parks.

Wood being the best plastic material made a present for the occasion;
They learnt it was traditional to lick twinklets on the first night,
recalling the bourganvillea crushed ice; still youthful, they sizzled,
being born in Panama but never having even been there.

The wedding ring was made of enamel video recordings,
and the honeymoon took two jade elephant steps.
It was known that the tallest mountains flew sideways
while they slept in tents of revolving doors.
The house sale weighed too heavy on her right ear.

But the lampshade made passionate love to the cashbook;
the tea poured out the cake and muffins for the accountants,
while film screens kissed her often, the dancers shouting curtains,
and the candle waxed lyrical about the nib's pet mouse
as it chewed the armchair's borrowed tuxedo.

The cloud fell on her toe, and climactic shifts
meant the anniversary had to take place in the cat basket,
leaving a large indentation on her white whiskers,
and the delicious iron filings filled everyone's exploded noses.

They lived remotely ever before, casting
against the tide of foam that meant the house was inside out
forever. The children stuffed themselves with olive chocolate to
keep warm outside, and fell asleep to the violent roar of owl droppings.

Jonathan Morley

Swimming Lesson
for Eleri

the beeches golden
  a crocodile of children
crunching on coxes
  your eyes a vixen's
brown and black, new like conkers
  emerging from shell

St. Ives, Cambridgeshire: a History

As I was going to St. Ives
I met a man with seven wives.
Said he, 'It's really much more fun
Than having only one.'
   – Roald Dahl

Strong men have blanched, and shot their wives,
Rather than send them to St. Ives
   – Rupert Brooke

By the river folk say you can't judge a book by its cover,
and only a fool parts with his money too quick.
The monks said the bones in the churchyard were those of St. Ivo

and covered him back up in his grave, the dirt like a glove,
the one that delighted baby Jesus with his tricks,
who flew on a carpet from lands where they have seven wives-o,

heard about the market when he stopped off to buy fags at Dover
and decided to wait here for his final heart attack,
for it's a comfortable green town, hand in glove with the river.

Pilgrims came from miles around, from Royston and Shelford and Over,
and local shops sold out of golden rings and wedding cake
where the Saint's bones pardoned sinners for a fiver.

Now I'm very fond of my wife, but I wouldn't mind another
so, dodging the sirens and the weeds' cold snakes
I plunged into the river, and swam across alive-o,

but I found the men of St. Ives to be strong and faithful lovers,
the monastery dissolved c.1536.
I was not robbed of spending my damp fivers, however,
at Olly Cromwell's birthplace, the town of joie-de-vivre!

The Winter of the Modern Media

'But I propose a fresh matter of Britain'
  – Roy Fisher

We have sent our champions into battle
and, our blood up and our mouths steaming
we fuck off the cold: meat batches, curry pies.
We gird our loins.
Our eyes, ten thousand slippery alert footballs
flick convincingly from centre to wing,
many-mouthed, ant-brained monster,
making the rooftops echo
and the stands of our opponents tremble
with the rip in the air of our roaring
something's going to get smashed

head-high the wood's heart
glowing stop at a tree
we lopped a squash of
heavy crimson blobs
carried it away like a brain
between thin trunks
and over the papery leaves
now ghost of lichen only
sliced, oozing, you fried like meat
o bloody sweet gem

in an astonishing twist to the story
of the men of the south, denied work permits
and housed in Bristol until such time
as they can be deported, a splinter group
has commandeered barges and is rowing,
like the pikey, upriver towards Shrewsbury.
Dunkirk must have looked very much like this.
The men have hooked noses, beards, eyepatches,

turbans, scimitars, books of false prophets.
If you meet them do not speak with them,
lock your doors and alert the police.
Sources close to the Prime Minister hint
of an accommodation to be made with the rebels,
but regional chiefs in the Midlands refuse
to enter negotiations, saying that the Haradrim
must first curb the wantonness of their orcs.

The sun, a pale fluorescent orange,
like Orion threw a ball for Sirius
but the dog wouldn't go in the water to fetch it
so it sits glowing on a beach of mud.
You feel things more intensely as you grow old
and experience kindles inside your dirty shell,
oh, who am I trying to kid? Life danced away
like flames on the fire, empty packets of crisps,
and its shadows run over the wall of my eyelids.
What I mean to say is, I am old,
and I remember that we fought a War
to keep the British nation pure-pure.
Now it has been invaded by stealth,
and political correctness. Dark hordes
swamping our city with their gabbling words,
frying garlic in ghee, callaloo rice and peas,
masala fish on nan, the clean sweet scent
of halal meat, I'd sooner slit my throat,
and will, some day: I never vote.

Your face slashed white
and your eyes mauves,
like you've been painted
shite by the Fauves,
know this my love,
it causes hurt:
the man in blackshirt
has a black heart.

Sir, I write with a pinch of scepticism, a good splash of rationalism and a stout dose of common sense, on the subject of economic migrants. The hysteria of your correspondents notwithstanding, we all know that the history of these islands has been, with only a few blips, one of peaceful and ethnically stable farming communities, save for in the exposed easterly regions, since the second century, when Uther Pendragon beat back the Romano-Trojans, and can remain so. It would seem that, in a region ravaged by low wages the best solution would be, as always, to close our borders and allow for a good, healthy period of inbreeding. Yet our vacillating and corrupt civic councillors will not grasp the Phoenix' tail, with the result of which we are all painfully familiar: ragtaggle bands of foreigners, marauding and pillaging at leisure, eating our swans and generally making a mockery of the honest yeoman who works all his life for a fraction of the money these squanderbirds receive in handouts. I and many of my friends have begun to question the worth of such foolhardiness, and our whispers are getting louder: 'tis said that in Hinckley horses are eating themselves.

Prince Is Muntjac. Full story revealed on page 12.
Gawain Thribble, a shoemaker's apprentice from up north
was cruising in the Binley Woods area yesterday
when he disturbed a herd of muntjac
led by none other than the godly Prince Ray,
the photogenic heir-apparent last seen
enjoying the gralloching of heretics at Sandringham,
Norfolk, this last Sabbath (right).
'He came up to me,' Thribble, 36, recalls,
'butting at my legs, fearsome little bugger he was
and I would have let him have it with both barrels
but then I realised his eyes were blue, and
he was scratching words with his horns onto the dirt:
I am the rightful born good king of Albion.
I was staggered, sorry, terrible pun.'
It appears there was a plot to supplant His Highness,
replace him with a faun, as popish a thing
as ever ran wild through the Forest of Arden

and rule through treasonous black magic.
The prime suspect in the press investigation
is a feminist, Donna Blitzen, from Pidley, Cambridgeshire.
Here I am, outside her hovel by the river,
but Ms Blitzen was not at home.
She has been a thorn in the authorities' side
for many years, unceasing in her demands
to ban page three girls and a tireless campaigner
on behalf of PEANIP, the East Anglian separatist party.
We out these easterners to be stinking Lollards
here photographed holding secret meetings
with a gang of marsh-wiggles from Norwich.

Something is rotten in the state of Mercia.
Isn't it interesting that these do-gooders who rush to the defence of immigrants always claim that they are fundamentally 'equal' to us, as if the fact that they are different automatically makes them nasty. How naïve! Am I alone in thinking that it cannot be mere coincidence when, on the one hand a black tide oozes up the Severn and on the other the crown prince is kidnapped by mammals of Oriental origin? She then goes on about the thuggery and violence we see all around us, paedophiles and soucouyants free to roam, serious breach of homeland security, political will of our leaders, etc. I have many friends who are muntjac and know them to be a rude and warlike race – yet they are not our kith. To the blissed-out pinkoid-liberals whose whingeing stifles these pages I say, yes, we all should be less tolerant of caballers who would sell our once proud nation downriver for a fistful of cheese. And to anyone who comes a-knocking come election time, I advise you have an answer prepared to these questions: *how many muntjac are at large in the West Midlands* and *how many have AIDS and TB?* Otherwise go boil your head.

The fen, who is a she, blows,
and the road is never straight, except by ditches,
and buckles like a snake. The marsh shrugs.
Folk are weird out here, where the land thins,
the road signs rain: Mere Way, Splash Lane, Fen End,

villages camping on her rich black land,
people in mist. Nowadays, of course,
they're pushing up luxury riverside homes,
a high speed rail link, a science park, an airport,
but some fields you can't build on,
they flood in spring,
and one day water will cover it all again.
There's one place down the road
where you can hear the river rushing along under the high street,
another where it has a thirst and invades the beer gardens,
a drain where cars sink without trace.
Global warming, sea levels, these are issues,
solar panels on churches, maybe.
A damp seat of rebellion,
Boadicea, various beefy barons, then Cromwell,
then the draining of the fens.
We watch the gypsies, hold our tongues.

HOPE MAY BE at hoof for the young prince,
writes Poppy Pepper, our psychologist.
Cases of children cohabiting with
animals are rare, but not uncommon.
In the past people were brought up by wolves,
gazelles, goats, snails, eagles, chameleons…
Blushing, withdrawing into oneself, being
indicators not of a person's shyness
but of their beastly upbringing, or nature
doctors can sever the brain of Prince Ray
between the right and left cortex, putting
the muntjac to sleep, free his smooth body,
with no more pain than a cochlear implant.
Language imprints at age 2-6 months,
therefore, provided the prince undergoes
an intensive speech therapy course will
he soon resume his duties in the state
and utter kingly words: beef, mine, war, no?

Farmers call for an end to the ban on deerhunting.
The Home Secretary vows to catch the witch.
A fleet of dhows has reached as far as Redditch.

The traitors who call us racist
when we express legitimate opinions
about numbers of asylum seekers
hereabouts are Trots and bigots,
taking away the right to free speech.
I'm no racist, I hate Germans,
no, it's these people who are driving
us into voting BNP:
we've no other policies.

Now with 80 pages of sport and motors!!!
My loyal subjects, hosts of Nuneaton,
our most welcomed guests, the Haradrim
and you gentlemen of the press: salaam.
Brownbaked features will place one only
in hell's mid-circles, and it is with joy
that we announce the new entente
twixt the Arabo-Africans and us.
The purpose of this summit is joining
agin the common foe, not to mention
that, as an ageing kingdom, we need
a cheap domestic workforce for hoisting,
spooning and dressing, wiping and washing:
refugees from Norfolk. By 2050
we will have melted the polar icecaps,
flooding that marshy county; their doge,
Hereward, in the Isle of Ely
seeing which way the tide is rising
a slimy army hath sharked up.
Puddleglums, Gotobeds, Sméagols and Déagols
are even as we speak paddling westwards
via nasty, damp sluices, culverts and dykes

in order to make a preemptive strike
on our pastures, and the white hills of your missus,
intelligence informed us this morning.
Imagine webbed fingers around your neck,
cold lips sucking at your eyes, comrades,
Anglian terrorists weaving their spells,
morphing you into a heron, or eel
& fear not glorious death in this bloodbath!
To the A14! We dine on flish tonight!

Thus we sent our champions into battle
and, our blood up and our mouths steaming
we fuck off the cold: meat batches, curry pies.
We gird our loins.
Our eyes, ten thousand slippery alert footballs
flick convincingly from centre to wing,
many-mouthed, ant-brained monster,
making the rooftops echo
and the stands of our opponents tremble
with the rip in the air of our roaring
something's going to get smashed
smashed
sma-ashed
son you're going to get smashed!

Alan Mumford

From the guidebook On Galbi

At sunset the sky is the colour
of a lemon's skin. Imagine too
the sand being the same colour. Imagine
how the fabled buildings on the fabled hills
on Galbi glow at sunset as turquoise as flames
in advertisements for drivefuels.

The surface of each object has a thin blue rim.
The sun stretches the shadows of the rose-smugglers
and the rose-mongers to where the black women
move their hips to their music. There is a sadness
on Galbi. Liken it if you like to garden history
after 1910, or silver-surfaced wood,
or the beauty of carpets destroyed
in 1939, or the architecture of museums
which, however beautiful, are prisons.

On Galbi the summers are spent watching
the beautiful flight of the beeli-hawks
and the fluttering progress of the pollenwings.
In winter the branches of the apple are bare.
Liturgical songs issue at the appointed times
from the neon-lit praying stations. Now and then
tens of thousands die in tribal wars; afterwards
the elders honour the sacrifices of the killed
in empty ceremonies, and the quality of the smiles
of the elders on Galbi are studied for meaning.

How (it seems) I came to be tattooed
in the house of W★★★★ R★★★★
in the Old City of Jerusalem

It was the sour stench of tear gas
rising up the steps of David Street
from the alleys of the Christian Quarter.
It was the Border Guards beating
their prisoners after Friday prayers.
It was the blueness of sky,
it was the air-powered hiss of bus doors,
it was *dein goldenes Haar, Margarete.*
It was a haircut at the barbershop
in the Muslim Quarter,
it was the date (1714)
on the ironstone house
in which my father was born.
It was Karl Marx writing
that the worker has no homeland,
it was the failure of the Enlightenment,
it was the McMahon correspondence,
it was the Balfour Declaration,
it was a Yemeni girl on Kibbutz Shomrat.
It was the coastal plain seen
from the Galilee highlands,
it was arriving in Nazareth,
it was tomatoes growing in sand
in the Wilderness of Zin,
it was George McRae singing *Rock your baby.*
It was the gold teeth of Bedouin girls,
it was *kif* on the Lebanese border,
it was the greyness of England,
it was looking for work in Tiberias.
It was her name scratched on a hotel wall,
it was passing through deserts in buses,

it was the rest-stop near Yad Mordechai,
it was a signpost to El Arish,
it was the panic of an animal in front of a fire.
It was the indiscriminate pursuit of affection.
It was the footsteps of a priest.
It was mist at dawn on the Jaffa Road,
it was the stars seen from the desert at night,
it was the chemicals in the hair dye,
it was the sound of earth landing on the pine.
It was the strength people need.
It was the evening
and the black walls of the passageway.
It was the blind man on the Via Dolorosa,
it was *haji* painted above the shop doors,
it was the mother suffocating her baby
to protect it from *fedayeen*.
It was not knowing the names of trees.
It was being afraid of snakes,
it was not knowing the names of birds,
it was organophosphates in the orchard,
it was poor sight in the dark,
it was the mirrors turned to the wall,
it was the streetlamp's small circle of light.
It was the loneliness of people who believe they believe,
it was the hopelessness of choirs,
it was the smell of stone and wood in churches.
It was the callousness of killers,
it was the casual cruelty of soldiers,
it was arrested development,
it was abortions we procured.
It was Graham who died at four,
it was the fearful child's bedroom,
it was the abusive neighbour,
it was everything that has ever happened.

Recipe

Hesitate, then hesitate again. When
it is much too late... say the day before
the flight... tell her everything; tell her
about the letter you never sent,
about how the words gathered a grey sheen
from rubbing against the coins and keys
in jacket pockets all through the summer
and autumn and winter of that year.
Make it clear that this all happened long ago.
Tell her that you let this love grow more heavy
until it was *round and without limit.*
Hand her the words as in-flight luggage,
give her an extra squeeze at the boarding gate,
and say *'see you whenever, maybe never.'*

Waiting for the Magi in the Rhondda Valley

To catch the sun and light the strands of straw
to make a proper fire to keep them warm
they could have used her mirror or the glass
from broken bottles in the underpass.

But that would risk smoke, and from the hills
which dwarf the town the watchers for miracles
and reincarnations of tribal gods would see
and seek them out and kill the baby.

In any case, the sun is rare in winter
over Pontypridd. He tells the mother
the appearance of the red-breasted bird
each morning means their prayers have been heard.
The kings from the East he's seen in dreams
will come to Taff Street, over the hills and streams.

At Gaza

The city with its beaches of forgetting
and continuous strands of memory
is woken by the waiter of history
with a bill for its own bloodletting.

Document all; don't discard in despair
the notes from the prison cell or the shapes
of the contours on our maps, or our shops
and cafes. Breathe. Breathe the city's air.

Coin a phrase to capture the colour
of her eyes which have lately excited you
to dreams of struggle – call it *lagoon blue*.
Include it on your banners in her honour.

Keep her with you – in a drop of the sea –
in a strand of her hair – time's singular *we*.

Pottery shard (undated)

Every day we ate salmon, the dried stuff... red.
The fires on the hill burnt all week, the wind
Fanned the flames, your wounds healed. You said
The creature was extinct and we'd never find
Our way out of the valley. You were half right.
We left you there in that god-forsaken far country,
Buried you with your shield at first light,
Moved west, covered our tracks at every
Turn in the trail. Once we saw smoke, a red
Flag fluttering in a clearing, and on the wind
Was the smell of roasting. Healer said
We should risk contact. That week he went blind
And died. We buried him by a tree.
By the second moon we reached the sea.

In The Valley of the Nobles at West Thebes

'Over there Flaubert once ate his breakfast
where Americans now bitch about the heat.'
The guide squats, makes a drawing in the dust
of the ear-ringed cat goddess, Bastet,
which by dusk will be sand on the breeze.

The tourists, sun-struck mercenaries far from home,
stumble like Pharaoh's captives on the frieze.
They arrive in battered taxis which come
down these roads, these paved bones of armies,
to stare blankly at the walls of hieroglyphs.

The sleep of the preserved and bandaged dead
continues far from the Tomb of Vines.
They lay in glass cabinets now in these folk's towns.
Their mouths are opened, imploring, not for bread.

Candy Neubert

reef

You have shown me the other look of things.
How, when I am on my back in water
I am spreading rudimentary wings –
how, by turning over more, a sort of
dorsal fin rises out of the surface,
breaking the bitterly bright skin of it.
Then the other skins break, and in each place
we were held in, we spill shockingly out.
You let me see you where I don't have eyes,
longer and more accurate than eyes see,
breathing until it hurts into the light,
darker and darker. You point out to me
what men have though of as a hole, in fact
is not a hole at all, but a flat cleft.

desert

I'll not desert you he said from the bathroom but
not saying it to her face letting the words drop
in her ear letting them fall over the door like
simple things like I'll have soup for lunch like
it might rain today she let them fall around her
head and picked them up and kept them years and
years I'll not desert you he said walking through
Gate 4 she wore them round her neck at first then
pressed them in a book I'll not desert you straight
from Mills and Boon not that he read any of that
she took them out on summer afternoons the words
like nettles gently stinging it was good for her it
kept her wary when she read de*sert* it was a *des*ert
with a mirage of oases when she saw the words had
faded like the small black legs of spiders she could
learn to recognize those kind of words in other
mouths like I am not that sort of man for instance

facing west (yin)

You're there outside the house (yang),
a paintbrush in your hand,
the sea (yang) fifty yards away
and a hot, bright sky (yang).
You've painted pitch (yin) on the walls
and now it's just the chimney – high (yang).

He said he'd help,
come out (yang), up (yang),
but inside (yin), he is asleep (yin).
You hesitate (yin), then you climb
and dip the (yang) brush into pitch (yin).
Inside (yin), he's sleeping (yin).

Perhaps you're back in bed with him
or make him toast and honey (yin),
or tea (yin) with two sugars (yin).
Perhaps you sit there on the sand
until he's up and out at last
and in his car, and drives off, fast (yang).

porch

You said if I were safely married, you'd hang out
at the bottom of the garden. How many houses sleep
with no lights on? Now, though someone speaks poems
in my ear, I hear the sound of your feet scuffing
in the porch, and the quiet whistle under your breath
sounds as if there are children playing outside.

one machine may block another

in my head imagining as I do the exact place
where you sit in the afternoon sun
its white light flat on the side of your face
and the Anglepoise on the desk head on

where you sit in the afternoon sun
the index finger of your right hand cocked
and the Anglepoise on the desk head on
your palm swirling the little plastic box

the index finger of your right hand cocked
your body staring at the screen not just your eyes
your palm swirling the little plastic box
sitting on the edge of the chair as if to dive

your body staring at the screen not just your eyes
the whole room humming balefully at you
sitting on the edge of the chair as if to dive
while all the phone says in my ear is   oo   oo   oo

the whole room humming balefully at you
its white light flat on the side of your face
while all the phone says in my ear is   oo   oo   oo
in my head imagining as I do the exact place

sentences

1

Let one of them begin to grow a beard.
Let him be taken into the Hindu
Kush and then left there for a week to fend
for himself. Give him a cup and a few
pieces of flat bread that look like leather,
and for cover a heavy coat with long
sleeves intended for the mountain weather,
as the people of that region wear. On
cold, starred nights let him stare into a new
heaven – ridge after ridge endlessly far,
split by green torrents. Perhaps a guide who
says nothing, speaks no English, has no car,
has never seen a car. Perhaps no guide
at all, just the vast world on every side.

2

Let the other remove his beard; also
his turban, and take the robe from his back.
Replace it with a T-shirt. Let him go
out into the high straight lines and tarmac
of New York to live there for seven days
as best he can. On cold, electric nights
let him seek a quiet place. Let subways
swallow him. Let him gaze up at the bright
orange sky, perhaps from a station bench
at midnight. Let him feel himself alone
in the multitude. Give him a few cents.
On second thoughts, tell him to find his own.
Then let them meet on neutral ground between,
and seat themselves, and let the talk begin.

his son's mouth

Watch how his lips uncurl. They are
toffees filled with little burrs,
hoisting the red flag of his mouth.

One day his women
will be banana leaves furled open
from their soft white cores,

one day they'll eye him doubtfully
as he smoothes shaving cream
in snow all over them,

his lips apart and concentrating,
pulling them down tunnels,
plucking seaweed on the way.

Just like his father. The hearts
of engines break over the floor,
whispering: here we are, we are yours.

Blobs of Swarfega glisten on the wall,
following their blood line, asking for
tea, two sugars, ready to start sucking.

the horses

The horses have always been good to me,
and the old pony with the yellow teeth.
I move them round from field to field,
slip halters, shut the gates, make mud.
The trough with weed is like a jellied back
I can slap gently with a flat hand.
Take out a scoop and the next day
there is no hole.

The horses look after me but not him.
I am a fat adolescent in his house
and steal the chocolate.
I am a fine girl; he has affinity with me.
The walls are plastered with his shots.
He hides the chocolate until he feels
like giving it, which is not often,
and it's no good then.

The horses are good to me, still.
Still, in the green square of their home,
they quietly eat.

The horses carry me when I ask,
and then restore me whole. He takes me
over and over; I am filed away
under the correct date. Like horses
I have a big body and a small head
and I pull the grass and move slow,
like water, though I could
gallop fast.

if I could thank you it would be for

your poise your shoulders your last kiss in the doorway
of the house where I stayed your voice your dark suit
long thighs veined hands the poem the way you read the
poem your ease with your nakedness while you made tea
the umbrella you carry the helping hand always ready the
press of your leg against my foot your hands your voice
your containment being there when you said you would
your coming with me so easy and willing your hands your
disbelief your confidence your weight on me your thigh
moving mine apart your difficulty with being a good man
your looking at me your melt into me the layers of your
clothes shirt jacket coat my hands inside them your voice
your firmness your laughing your listening the way I miss
you your hands your voice your look straight at me across
the room the time you didn't touch me all the time you
touched me the way you read the poem your not having a
drink first the veins on your hands your strong thighs
your happiness your remembering everything

leaving queen street

I thought it was your mattress
leaving the house
which was the main part of your life, gone.
Someone bought it, you said.
I thought of the big soft square unsteadiness of it
heaving off the bed, tackling the corner,
knocking your change or the bowl
or whatever it was
off that little window sill
at the top of the stairs;
I watch it humping down those stairs
making your eyes water
taking your marriage, your affairs, me,
my bad back,
right through the kitchen
ducking its head, out.

Linda Rose Parkes

The Distant Aunt

She'll ride in from the Ice Mountains,
mists dragging her rough cloth
where she's concealed a purse of coals
to trade for whisky, a tot of milk.
Steam still rising off her pony,
I'll smooth clean sheets for her,
shake out a duvet.

There'll be hammering across the street,
voices and music from a radio
as she stands in the middle of the room
and we converse with signs.
A gesture comes to mean
the laundry, bitter herbs,
desire for chestnuts.

Not everything will be easy:
her toilet habits, her neglecting
to flush; the way she messes up
the towels, shares my jewellery –
and when friends drop in
makes such complicated drinks
(as if it were they who'd trekked miles across snow plains)…

Some days I'll miss the instant foods,
the shelf life of a few minutes;
hours carefully cordoned off
with a rush in between
which keeps things moving.
She has no signs for tired or late.
We wake in a loose expanse of trust,
studded with light and sudden
winds which blast the roof
or spread the pollen.
I start a thought and keep crossing
back for a set of instructions,
a dropped notebook: as if I was
charting a lost self

who'd set off for the mountains
with provisions,
an indelible memory
for maps. Even the crumbs
on the formica, the amber liquid
in the glass, will be fresh events
in an old country.

Nanny's Coffee

Every young girl crazy with pain
would find solace in Nanny's roomy girth,
the thick aroma of exhortations
to put some blood back in the veins

by drinking *le bon café, noir et sucré*.
Now, if *you* were Antigone,
this coffee might throw the tale
off course, pulling you to the roof

of your mouth, the needy furze
at the back of the tongue.
With coffee warming in the hearth,
you could find yourself starting

to be lulled by the sight of the steam,
the sound of Nanny's voice,
feel of her housecoat pressed
to your cheek. For you, hope never has fled

that far – so far you couldn't call it back
with the thought of a party, a new dress,
the handsome bloke who's bound
to glance your way.

But imagine: the flagstones, winter and cold,
cold morning after days without sleep;
your rebel brother rotting on the road
and no one else to bury him against the king's edict.

Our heroine knows she has no choice
but to be entombed with him.
Le sale espoir! This kidding oneself.
And look at Nanny –

all love and anguish as she bellows
the fire, grabs the pot. You can taste
her sweat from where you're sitting
as daybreak filters through the room.

Her roughly swept back hair falls
loose over one eye and she pushes it
behind her ear.
No thoughts but for Antigone;

that stubborn girl will break her heart.
But no – it must not come to that!
Drink, ma petite, come warm yourself!
Let sleep gloss over ugly times. What's done is done.

Single Frame

        She sits *just for a moment till father gets home.*
I count the buttons, chase the stitches;
the colour of my mother's cardigan
is rose granite in the early evening
when sun washes deep inside the stone.
        Nixon smirking on the telly,
she sips her tea. Through the open curtains
dusk bathes the grass; beneath the sill
a stack of records: Mario Lanza, Joan Hammond
whose plush cleavage, full red lips, turn
        my attention back towards my mother,
who each time I look grows more ephemeral
in her cardigan with the crocheted stitch,
the lavender tinge of Yardley's talcum
breathing from her pores.
        The me tucked inside her arm is a freckled
blur against the backdrop as I struggle
to make out what age I was or whether
I was there at all with the full-blown
roses swaying in the rug.
        Yet this image which pushes to the surface
at three in the morning when I'm trying
to sleep, fetches in me what I think
I knew then, at the moment
I first understood it.
        I see how the wool chafes my mother's skin,
her breasts are dwindling
beneath the buttons, while her collar bone,
a bleached necklace, is papery-thin,
brittle with longing.
        I can hear a language stalled in her blood

like dust and air and spools
of dark crowding the lens
with the loose-covered chairs,
the polished coal bucket.

The room flies apart
reassembles
brighter now
around the edges
as if the touchpaper's about to catch.

In the Beginning was Menses

Her blankets thrown carelessly back one morning
He was taken off guard, realised
how close to the surface blood was.

Sun scooped the washline of cottons but He felt bewildered:
how to handle the heart always pumping.
And the skin stretched transparent over the raw.

It wasn't exactly what He'd had in mind
with all His careful scrapings, His discrete particles.
Salt molecules, atoms of stars,

all those early mornings and late nights
sieving the air – for qualities of light and photosynthesis –
through an oak-leaf colander.

How had He failed to make allowance for such quantities
of blood? He started to dread spills; didn't have the stomach
for the production of knives, nuclear fission, accidents with harpoons.

Squeamish about bleeding from inside,
He worried a lot about women's menses, the shortness of cycles;
was bothered by smell, the messy tampons

or babies' heads crowning, tearing the tissue.
He hadn't anticipated the way things would leak
and was growing desirous of

odd socks snitched on brambles, millions of trees
blowing; a woman's sheets tugging at pegs,
tangy as lemons and best weather

for running to the top of the hill; lazing all day,
flat on His back pretending clouds are horses.
There was much more pain than He'd imagined.

The Punter

Let's say I start with sky. A layer of cirrus, some scud
shafted with light. But this isn't about weather
or where I happen to be going when I see this hard-bitten,
sixty-something bloke in his auto, listening to a song on the radio.

This is about how I make him listen, close:
I want a lover with a slow hand. I want a lover with an easy touch.
Get him to say things like: 'I'll give you one anytime, you tart'.
Make him wonder what happened to the old tunes

before I interview his wife and all his lovers to conjure up
a loss, a life passed by: *not come and go in a heated rush.*
No silks, oysters, no talented foreplay, this is about me sifting
an image of rough hands, importunate pricks;

sorry fucks enacted in minutes of waking or falling back
to sleep. At the same time knowing the moment of lift,
the real scoop to fetch sighs, is always, but always, the discovery
of treasure, buried hours of gold showering sparks.

But herein lies the danger: loose a creature in the forest,
you have to track, leave the path, till you're no longer familiar
with the habits of trees, the tread of soil,
when the creature changes

into rarer furs, indigenous to shadow. And even if the bloke
appears to remain seated, once he's spotted the punter,
he does a bunk, stashing the dross along with the gold,
the song almost finished.

Which brings me face to face with my own slim knowledge
of the heart in its electric skin, the spine live with static.
Music of the groin, ecstasy of quim, when they're loved
just right.

The Curator

Yet here I am, gazing through an old window
of a gabled house with intricate glass doors
cased in iron flowers.

On the inside, a set of porcelain galleons
you wouldn't remember. One in particular,
redolent of indigo, moss, ochre.
Next, the bottles carefully labelled.
Item 1: Memory of Conversation
          Outside The Cathedral in Winter.
Item 2: Colour of Your Eyes Remembered
          On Copse Path Through Fronds and Mixed Ferns.
Items 3, 4 and 5: Mixed Juices, Flowering Magnolia.
          Hands Travelling between Thigh and Navel.
A series: Spats, tied up in muslin,
scented with pot pourri.

But the knowledge of your former heart,
freckles on left breast, bushel of belly,
vagina with its folds of blackness –
I've stowed faithfully
in silent vats.

Every day I walk the great halls,
lyrical, confiding, given over to tears,
sometimes to scorn.
Of all the treasures in the storehouse,
I don't intend to let go
of that galleon. I clean the rigging,
dream of setting sail
one day, in fair winds.

Forfeit

Your remaining knight whispers:
one day he'd like to fall in love,
sip tall beer under the stars, watch the sun rise
with that someone when branches reach
into the wind and rooks are flying
to the rook house, come to hold parliament
in trees, amble in the spidery grass.
About to close his fingers on your Queen,
the Chess Master leans across the squares.
What exactly does the loser forfeit?

Mornings, when light swims
to the roofs and you stand for minutes
at the window, held by crocuses and frost?
Sex, its slow breeze patterns,
the shadow that falls across the path
between the drainpipe and the blackberry bushes?
Saturday night's piss up?
You can let that go.
Your flat screen
or your new windows,
your sandwich
or your good coat?
The woodlands,
the hills,
the oceans,
the last bus
crashing its gears down familiar streets?

You try to divine the opponent's mood,
embrace the strategies, have one of your own
and two up your sleeve, a triumphal plot.
But the souls of the rooks have already nested.
High over the board their wings beat
and the black knight gallops
to the shoreline:
beads of water hang in his mane,
a curtain of surf blows around him.
One forward, two sideways,
one sideways,
two back.

Jane Routh

The Red Cow

They were reaching north up the coast
for shelter in the lee of Skye,
stiff with cold after another day
of stinging rain and waves so short
and steep they'd had to take
every sounding more than once,
when the last of the squalls raced away east,
washed the sky to that pale clear blue
that fades to green near the horizon
and a brief evening sun poured colour back
into the sea, so they all saw it:
a cow, two cables off on the starboard quarter,
sitting on the waves and chewing a cud of tangle,
the curve of her spine and bony haunches
darker than a Hereford's, a rich red
among the *Glas Eileans* and the *Sgeir Dubhs* –
a single eccentricity in their meticulous work
and unremarked by the Hydrographer.

Mealista

Miles down the road, miles
past the last ruin,
where the single track road
falters into wheel tracks
through bog, and the coastal strip
narrows to an insufficiency
before bony mountains crowd the sea,
close the gate against the wind:

there's a broken chain on a mooring ring
and a concrete slip runs out into the water,
as if it were natural to walk the length
of a dead end road into the sea,
as if you could keep on going
to Cape Breton, Newfoundland, Australia.

MN 546 711

You'd expect sand, champagne-and-honey colours
out here on the edge of the west
but on this dark-floored beach, feet slide off grey cobbles
that knock as if the world beneath were hollow.

Boulders of seal-smooth basalt and no beachcombings
– except my one handful of shells: a limpet,
a topshell with the paint worn off, three winkles
and a diagram on my finger end, a Moebius strip of coral.

Let's say the Atlantic Conveyor swept it here
from Bonnaire, one fragment broken off the reef
when a fisherman dived to check his rudder
in the sheltered green water of the salt shallows,

and you can see why I hoard it like a magpie
with gold: the world's still working.

On the Island

Such a morning, and everyone with the same idea:
a neighbour in orange oilskins scrambles
down the foreshore and hauls in a small red boat.
The washing's out at Carminish.

Starlings on the fencewire pitch in the breeze
above grass studded blue with devil's bit.
You can see the houses on Ensay; soon they'll fade
in mauve haze warming up from the south.

Two pairs of ring netters out in the Minch
dance on a sea the blue of postcards.
I can hear the ferry's engines slowing down
between the reefs by Killegray.

They are the Happiest People wrote Martin Martin
but know it not. That was 1697.
It's what travellers to islands always say,
or something like it – and then move on.

The bus driver leans out of the window to talk
to the cousin he's not seen for a week.
A red van is blocked, then three cars.
Nobody minds. The van driver reads his paper.

Seven of the moorings you can see from the house
were empty when I got up this morning.
Time to peg the washing out; time
to signal what I know with yellow towels.

Lineaments of an Afternoon

A single track road
 so little used, drifts of white sand blank it off

A walk
 over machair to the sea; orchids and meadow rue

A wide concrete jetty
 ungrasped handrails and unworn steps

A steep scend
 up the channel, calming in the island's lee

A sand bar
 across the narrows: turquoise, emerald

A narrow path
 nothing more than a sheep track into the hills

An old sore
 weeps a little even in a drying wind

A camera
 zipped into a pocket unused

A map
 unfolded

A bee

The Price

Evenings, I drive the geese up near the house.
I sleep with the window wide, though it's cold.
It's only half-sleep, half my brain's listening;

listening for a change of tone (they murmur
most of the night, on and off), listening for wingbeats,
for whatever danger sounds like.

Alarmed, I've run into the field three nights this week.
There's so much dew, it's like wading
through shallow water back to bed.

Down ripples in the grass, even in still air:
perhaps it's this makes you disbelieve a creature's
dead. Why do they take the heads?

John says you can call foxes up:
Shine a light in their eyes, and squeak.
I practise: suck hard on the back of my hand.

He says I'll need to stay very still,
draw it in close for a gun like mine.
He says I should buy a rifle.

All My Dead

The lately-dead return in the night, balance
their over-large heads on thin bones and ask
Do you think I am going to die? Yes, I say, Yes.
Their faces are crumpled like a newborn's.
I hear them screaming under the bed.
It is not easy to imagine what it is like
to exist only in someone else's memory.

The long-dead are quieter. They leave their toils
in ones and twos, step up to say their names.
Sometimes they bring a landscape with them.
Souls of their dead infants cling to the womens' skirts
like patchy fog; even they do not remember
their faces. Subsistence is what they care about:
they do not mind what you invent.

And those not-yet-dead who know they
are next in line, the ones with grandchildren,
make ready, and talk among themselves about
how someone should have photographed
the moor before it was fenced, or haytime even:
this is the closest they come to saying
what they mean. Then they start to repeat themselves.

The Elizabeth Ann
to Great Grandfather

Now all the other visitors have left
I can hear the ache of parched timbers.

Look: here I am on CCTV
running my hand along the strakes
and tapping on the copper nails
you hammered in.
New warps are neatly coiled along her decks.

Listen: the alarm; uniformed footsteps
running up the stairs. Too late:
my foot's on the gunwale,
I'm on board,
pull the tiller over hard.

She casts herself off.
                        The Haven unsilts.

I gybe and ease the sheets,
and sails that have hung slack
in the airless hall for years
gulp salt air   and belly out
in the following wind.

She storms through the Hessel Whelps
for the open sea. There are no charts
for sands that shifted then
but who cares, who cares,
it's in the blood. Isn't it?

The River Pilot's Wife

Come up the embankment: this is where
she would have watched for ships that flew a pilot's flag.

Look, back there, that's Read's Island, where he'd show her
the mandarin ducks' nest. Every spring as long as she can remember

lifting her to the bank to keep her skirts dry. Bending the reeds
for her to see. She always knew she would marry Isaac.

He'd row over to Paull to fetch her boiled shrimps; she stole
copper nails for him in her apron pocket from her father's yard.

Her girl's pride whenever she picked out a white-and-red flag
on a ship in Brough Roads. She was 15 when he kissed her.

Imagine her two months married and walking up here as if to meet him.
She can count on one hand the nights he has spent in her bed.

Just before dusk, like now, she hears the whistles and groans of waders
among the skypools and purple shadows on the mudflats

and she hears again his mothers' warnings: truant on that raft in the creek,
never a dry garment on him, out all day and out all night;

his own stories of current and tide, captains looking out for him,
and that leap from the deck, in the wind, in the dark: that leap.

She knows her own nights and days governed by moons, her own tide
turned, that flood of expectation now ebb and the fear of loss

and as she stares into the night, every star and its reflection
is signalling demands for a pilot to come on board.

Eleventh Hour
Armistice Day 2003

There are leaves still on the trees
near the mountain hut, Mont Blanc framed
perfect against blue sky. In Yellowstone
you can see only stars. It's night
in Auckland too: those are its lights
glittering across the bay from Devonport.

The South Pole's out of action, all turbulence
and wind. Mawson Station's on:
portacabins in primaries, rock, snowdrifts.
No one outside. Pale sky almost green.
Ascencion looks abandoned: 27° — dawn I think —
a white dory pulled up the hard, a wave.

Macquarie's frozen, a Sisley of lilac
greys and green, but Antarctica's left behind
its sound effects: sea ice breaks and cracks
unstoppably, a Weddell seal yawns.
Nothing from Nuuk; and in the dark, Denali's
lost to Anchorage's light pollution.

Ah yes. Bagdhad. Out-of-date
as you'd expect. A green shop sign,
an ordinary side-street. No one's about.
The text is Spanish — if I have it right, it says
all people are collaterals.
Everyone. Everywhere.

Sreejata Snyder

Coalescence

'A few more years, a few more ghosts to embrace'
  - Yusuf Komunyaka

Inside Tates' turbine room, I am
sandwiched between dysfunctional machines.
Rain smatters glass. I thought my skin had forgotten
the sudden cleansing of the dive,
hands reaching for the floor of the pool
the CESC children swam in. Only us,
not outsiders, who went down to the river.
Something here smells of coal. Always gritty, coated
with the coal dust in the air, we were
told to bathe thrice a day, all summer.
We didn't recognize the words in our mother-tongues,
confusing dirt with tint of skin. We were children
of the CESC, convent-educated, playing
in knee socks and organdie dresses,
our days dotted with tennis matches
and rose walks, gardeners and maids'
brushes walloping brown

lignite off door-meshes in clouds.
Clouds that returned to powder our limbs
after each bath. We plunged into the pool,
making the powerhouse chimneys bob in surprise.
Where does the coal smell come from? We would swim
like tadpoles, our washed skins turning
browner in the sun. Mothers yelled from verandas:
'five more minutes' as Zareen stroked the water back.
I can hear it lap against the edge as she swims.
Seven-year-old Buba dives so hard from the top board,

her underwear floats away amidst our shouts;
she swims, her white chemise a scrap of sail.
A few more years and she will have it right.
Nothing keeps us from the pool; not frogs coming back
despite the increased bleaching powder;
not snakes, which nest under the deep-end stairs.
Our arms return to wave, legs ceaseless as we disappear
into the dark, invisible bottom.

CESC: Calcutta Electric Supply Corporation, a British company, until recently.

Behind this eye…

You come on your Yezdi,
knees pointing
in two directions. The 'V'
of your shirt signifies:
dusk is a mantle
on your shoulders,
my arms are around you
on the bike and the engine throbs
like heartbeat. 'Hold on'
you say but we are
away.

★★★★

Inside this window
between the wire mesh
and the metal grill
a red-cheeked bulbul pair
have nested. You pass
my old place you say
and sigh.

★★★★

Oh God, Oh God
where does this one
come from,
clutching with its windows,
like someone else's dreams
I will inhabit?

★★★★

We walk down East Street
eating iced, orange lollies.
We have bought a cake
at Baker's Basket. You take
a photo of the bougainvillea tree,
mauve flowers nestle
on my art deco blouse,
trailing up the stone wall.

★★★★

On the bench
where we twine
our arms together,
look: a letter.

★★★★

That house had grilled windows
which sent away the river.
The morning
ferried school children
to the other side.
I could imagine
their voices, their hands
dipping in water.
Gentle ripples
breaking on the shore
two lawns away.

★★★★

We played with the Russian doll
in grandma's cupboard
on Sundays. You took its head,
I, its stiff skirt,
You pulled
another head off and me
a skirt, until we had them,
a line of faces
on your side, skirts on mine
like soldiers going to war.

****

In all your paintings there is
a bird that hovers
over cliff tops and pine trees
or wisps of smoke
that wane
away in the sky.

****

I too have dwelled
in sad places. The old banyan tree
at school that made the dark
look brown. I could hardly bear
to look at it, the fingers
rooted everywhere, the holes
in its trunk where things lived.
Its immense shade.

****

If I say 'I', I become
your grey mufti
or a maroon tie.
A walk by the flower stalls
near West End, a café
while it pours with rain.
Your steps on the stairs,
your dark brown eyes and
where was I?

Floating

The Victorian railings say it all: wrought iron roses
stretch your hammock tight, a tension as you sway,
pulling on a string. Paradoxes,
Danesh, how you would laugh
that moustache-curling laugh, that never ceased
to furl women into your charmed life.
                                              I need to deflect
my hunger
with batasas from Dorabjee
and your lemon-mint tea, to stand on Wadia rail bridge,
as the six o' clock to Bombay rushes by. You are lulled
to doldrums, dangling in your hammock, pulled
by the Mutha dragging into the dam.
You watch the projects spring up like mushrooms,
thinning out the wood, where roots go deeper each year
into eroding soil, hoping for an interruption
- an unexpected call from Malini,
perhaps from somewhere yet else - that would cut
the long string; the waiting; the drowning Mutha.

Batasas: a biscuit
Mutha: a river in Poona

The Kingfisher

'as if they were all one flesh, in a single dream,
and nothing to make them true, but space, and time.'
  – John Burnside

The day the big pine fell, missing us by inches,
we watched the kingfisher's slow swirl
over the broken stump. Mutely, it worked
a circle, all afternoon. 'Oh the poor thing', mother said,
coming out to see how far the sun came in.
If the railings stretched their full length in shadow
on the veranda floor, it would be
winter.
          Light, then shadow, inside the wafer-thin walls
of pine; layers of wood-lace, exquisitely fanned.
Our sheepdog ran to sniff at the termite-torn castle,
cocked a leg and went to look for the 'gecko' we tried to tame
with milk and eggs under the rose trellis. And still
the blue flight as dusk flushes over the river.
Mother will paint this, I thought, in her mind at least,
even if she stopped painting when I was born. 'Poor thing',
I hear her say, her eyes crinkled against the sun,
a breeze soft in her brown hair.

The timber people came from outside
Our gardeners wore grins
as they helped roll the logs away.
All winter they tended roses
beds of *Bianca* and *Black Prince*, but this was
a windfall.
          The hole filled with moon
in the dark. I willed the dancers to come out,
like always; there was no one. That night I dreamt
of maroon roses caught in porcelain bowls,
their fragrance elusive.

Split

I

The yellow balloons went bop-bop against the windows
as we drove away, everyone crying,
even my sister who had apologized
in advance for not being able to.
But we swathed vines and flowers everywhere,
quoted Ezekiel and Elizabeth Browning under the trellised arch
that threw a net of shadows on our faces so my father-
in-law had to tear the flimsy things down. They flung their arms wide,
mother, father, brother, his wife, child, two dogs. Tuesday dinners
at Grandma's, Sunday washing at Mom's
and supper when we all coalesced.
Two more weddings the same year, and I
in front of the mirror throwing handfuls of clothes
on the bed, trying on the white, then the blue with the hat,
a chiffon blouse, pink scarves, low and high heels. Even my own
parents forgot that I hadn't always been a part of the other
family. Across the continents our letters filled with news
of the last dinner, the dog fight, the length of Jake's runs,
news of a cousin stuck dumbfounded in Kuwait as the benevolent
troops lit up Iraq like a fourth of July.

II

Even the little boy on a fat pony in Darjeeling,
screaming for his mommy is a fixture. We came back
each summer, I explain, to the mall rounds,
the tea gardens dissolving into blue.
The lady in the pink saree has her hand raised
in an eternal wave, face clamped shut
against the boy's anguished cries: the Raj
tearing the jewel from it's heart,
dripping ghosts on our nights.

Look Jake, that silver in the distance
is China Peak, and that hill, Observation Hill; look
at my brown eyes in the mirror turn into mother's ice.

III

Now, we cut the cake – click - now we raise
our glasses – click - and now group photos please:
your mom and dad rainbowing; the grandparents
all in a row; there stands Reshmi with her first
smile after the heartbreak; Didi in her chiffon skirt;
the distinguished, dimpling justice of peace,
here's the whole family holding their breath, here's you
Jake, the tears still moist on your skin, your hair tousled
from the hug, your hesitant face,
all lit up, here's you, Jake, riven from the group
photo, from your mother's sap green dress. Click.

Subtracted Memory

The Hopi can disappear into jagged-faced rocks in the middle of plains and quiet pools of green waving with wild watercress. They can disappear – a generation or two, a family grazing sheep on a still autumn's day – into four-petalled squash-flower or cottonwood tree. They can loop between times, from now to not-now, fill their stories with wide-open mouths of clock-swallowing arroyos. The only constant: space: earth, the mother that gave them birth and waits to claim blood and bone back to loam. That is what you wished for, a constancy that blooms like a star; belonging that is timeless. Like survival at AFMC* which herds exceptions into flocks of junkies who sink into stellar visions, who flunk each year; which weeds from each batch the rough edged gift, all that does not fit. 'The difference is

of power;' you say, licking mayo off the burger, 'the difference between D. P. S. and St. Mary's'. How can I understand, perched on a bike in *Jaws*, where there is no un- belonging, where people hash and laugh over sex jokes on the notice board, negotiate 'well preserved' things, Yamahas, Enfields, Moments. There, I, inside the void, in a bomb-like contentment. You, dotting the margin, eyebrow raised for someone has said again: 'you sing beautifully'. You are unaware of bringing back the memory of love, singing like you do. A pause, then lights,

applause,

action:

cymbals, drum, electric guitar throbbing for a cue.

Then you,

on the plateau, singing as the first drops spill. Khanna curled into Reshmi's knee, feigning love, another Kapur. Reshmi, another me, feigning. I bend over to cover the guitar. Don't take it away; this moment will sustain a future. How ridiculous that I should race home, you perched on the back wheel. I didn't intend to come out of the bathroom and catch you stripping. Thank me when I take you home, 'beyond the call of duty', when

I revv and leave you rooted, on the parade ground. The story isn't about belonging anymore. 'Please

go,' you say, please understand.' Here comes your mother after the accident. She will hold you now, while the night stars. And you slip back to St. Mary's, the school for the gifted who give the world 'The Sound of Silence', the 'Nights of White Satin'; visions on a platter. While D.P.S. ploughs me. The last time we meet, a tension, as you beg for just one more, please. We don't know this is the last time. You thrust a picture of God into my limp hands as you leave; 'you need it,' you say, then, 'let me go, or I will be no different from them.' The Hopi belongs differently. A tension as we totter, pulled taut, like breath sucked in. Then you vanish, with the rest, into the squash-flower, petals pointing everywhere at the promise of night pooling over the parade ground walls,

where

the cattails

wave.

*AFMC is Armed Forces Medical College, a national institution. DPS: Delhi Public School.

Hover

The deluge sudden over trees, Mom in her housecoat running down the stairs to let the dogs in, shouting instructions to everyone to hurry, hurry, or we get caught. My sister slams shut her Grey's Anatomy, leans toward the river, saying everything can wait; even Ranikhet★. Mom runs, slams windows shut, says hurry. Father looks at the river with a gaze that longs to stay.

Rain turns the lawns to brown pools of mud. We watch the river rise, the paper folding sound not registering till my sister says look, oh look, then it is the rustle of silk sarees at a wedding. The sky turns green as the parrots fly by, so close we can see tucked up feet against white-feathered bellies.

Mom says hurry but we wait for the river dolphins. She can move tomorrow, or when the rain stops. The suitcases on the landing trip everyone up all afternoon. Then dusk, and another snatch of green. It's a female, high on the pine tree, sitting with its eyes closed, its neck exposed, as the blue-ringed male pulls its feathers free of rain. I watch father stroke Mom's hair once.

★Ranikhet, literally translating to "Queen's Garden," is a hill station in the Kumaon range of the Himalayas.

Frances Thompson

The Goat Bells

I want to know about the goat bells,
for their small hollow knocking is in my head.

I want to know if a bell
might be worn by many goats in succession,
if it might be generations, centuries old,
and if a child in the village might be wakened
by the same, the very same music
as was her mother, and grandmother, and great-grandmother.

I want to know about the bell-maker.
When he hammered out the tin cup
and hung the small clapper, did he test the bell
for tone and timbre, thinking maybe of a goat he knew,
so that when you open your shutters
and the light rushes in, and you hear
a near, familiar tapping and tocking,
you can say Ah, my goat, Maria, is there –
and did he die long ago, the bell-maker,
and do they remember his name in the village,
and is 'bell-maker' said along with his name,
and is a new baby sometimes called after him –

or are they disposable bells
that arrive in large boxes all the way from Athens
– or Tokyo?

I want to know what a bell means to its goat.
Do the bells at first drive the goats nearly mad,
and do they in the end settle for this madness

as they settle for the high winds
in the worlds where their clever feet take them
and the sweet still places they know
and the smell and scrunch of thyme
and the daily giving of the blessing of their milk –
and I want to know if, at the last,
it is the bell's kiss on the air
that betrays the goat to the man with the knife?

For the bell sounds the goat, its to-ings and fro-ings,
its choices and changes, and the silence of the bell
is the goat's musing and sleeping.

I want to know about the goat bells,
for their faint hollow harmonies are knocking
at the bowl of the mountains under the sun
against the silvered pulse of the sea.

Grace

When Dad said it before meals, it came
from his heart, for he loved his food and his God.
For us, bowed over our steaming plates,
grace was an exercise in patience. Sometimes
if we bothered to think, we might wonder:
Has everyone received the thanks that's due
for this coming-together of vegetables, roast,
the last-minute perfection of gravy? And what

of the clean, ironed cloth? – the pudding in the oven? –
the miracle of what we're about to leave
becoming tomorrow's what we're to receive?
Grace over, our mother's voice would break
the Amen's holy spell, with a question about
homework, or hockey teams, or washed hands.

What Thought Did

Thought went on a journey to the stars. When she got there, she kept on travelling beyond the stars, and even beyond that, and out beyond the beyond. Then, at the very edge of the universe, she came to a stop!

Thought knew it was the edge of the universe because she had reached a corrugated iron fence. Thought poked a hole in the corrugated iron fence to see what was on the other side. She peeked through, and saw – a feather.

Here is what Thought did. She poked a bigger hole in the corrugated iron fence, a hole big enough for her arm to fit through. She reached out for the feather, stuck it into the ground, and watched it grow. It grew into a hen.

After Thought came back home, she looked up at the stars, and she looked into the spaces between the stars, right out as far as the edge of the universe, remembering her journey, remembering the feather, remembering the hen.

Thought cannot remember where she stuck the feather into the ground. Was it on this side of the corrugated iron fence or the other? Is the hen outside the universe or inside it? Thought cannot see the hen. But she knows it is there.

Mrs Jones

These walls hold the business of the house –
they are marked by the red fingers of maids

who cut root vegetables; who kneel, at dawn,
at fireplaces. Listen

for the hollow slop of water-jugs carried up,
or chamberpots brought, at armslength, down

my long stairs, or the snap and chuckle
of a banister, where warm bodies might lean.

Mrs Jones lived here for ninety years,
and moved on long ago. Now she is back,

giving orders for a new look for the walls.
She has chosen a hand-painted paper

with leaves that twine and hide,
brown and black when I uncover them;

hints of skin on the air today; of breath
catching my own breath, blood on the tongue.

It is never quiet, this house of mine. Mrs Jones
has taken a lamp down to the cellar. She moves

the surfboards aside, to check on her preserves,
her jellies in jars, their low fires.

Ilfracombe

The streets, clean of summer's dross, are flapped out in the wind like ribbons. November afternoon is evening before you know it and by tea-time it's dark. I am climbing the hill, aiming for the top. Whew. I do not look down at the town – I look across at it, for the town itself is a hill. You might have stood here a few centuries ago in the scrub and wind and stared out at a black nothing on the sky. Now I can hold the constellation of the town in my palm. Stars spawn more stars. Business of living. Neighbours then the News and the kettle on. In the low space between us, one house holds open a bright rectangle in which red-carpeted stairs wind upwards. A mouse-click will take you to the top of them – click – the door creaks open and an ancient book lies, closed, on a table. Ignore it, look for the panel in the wall – click – it slides away and here is... a sunny garden with a fountain that throws out... a frog. A frog. Another frog. A key. Quick catch it; bad luck. Next time. Waste time with frogs. Catch the key. Look for the door in the garden wall, the door covered with trailing ivy pixels, the door that opens, that opens on to a high-resolution galaxy. In the middle, my house. My. There on another windy hill. Invisible ground floor. Study light on. My 60-watt window flames like Venus, like Betelgeuse, they can see it in Wales.

Beast?

What beast? Dark thing in your mind. It was a dark thing in my mind tore my sheep's throat out was it? Dark thing in my mind scared the living daylights out of my wife did it? Beyond the window a dark thing dissolves in wind and shadow. Now you see it now you. A dance of energy. Something like this happens we are all ripped. Scalded cat energy. Graceless scramble. Come on we are meant to be communicators but let's give the boys a language they understand simple go out and shoot it. Narrow boundary. Beyond the window a dark thing feeds, thin body absorbing living daylights, grunting, slurping, yawning, replete, making off along its own M25, the safe hedges, leaping across the plain of the B1431, in headlights that don't believe what they see. Saw. Oh yeah.

The History Lesson on the Shooting of Hostages

Imagine, says the teacher, *getting blood*
on your clothes from, say, a nosebleed
the magpie flops to the
pavement and
it jumps from the kerb to the double
yellow lines and
imagine how much blood how much more
blood would saturate

black head poking forwards poke poke poke
steps birdfooty along the double yellow lines
'saturate with blood' a thick military uniform
runs out across the road on its little machine
feet quite safely
in one day — and the killings lasted years
between the cars.

This was a so-called
'*comparison*'. A girl in a stripey scarf steps
out from between the pages of her closed
books and the magpie has flown away.
It, too, is history now.

Infinitives

To be scratched one day unaware
by the thorn,
to tend the tear;

to toss a coin;
to be hit by half a brick
in the middle of a song;

to trip on a straw; to be kicked
by a hen; to find
in one's own backyard, the stick;

or, at the party, to be resigned
to playing the spoons
and not at all to mind.

To touch stone.
To nudge the brute
in the bone.

To catch sight
of a splay of swans;
to note the sweet flute

fingered by the man
in the wheel-
chair, while the band

for once, is still;
to avoid the dreadful
dog that nips at the heels;

to play the game oh God
of Truth or Dare,
to scratch the head…

Li Po Sonnets

I

On the high Mara, to the west,
a distant storm is flashing.
The land, spotted like a leopard,
darkens, and the plain rustles.

A lone bull elephant appears
crashing from the undergrowth,
raises his trunk to trumpet in
the first sharp arrows of rain.

II

On a Bristol Channel sandbank,
stuck, with the tide ebbing fast,
wind rising, flares shoot to the sky,
the masthead signals Mayday.

The coastguard orders 'Lifeboat launch!'
Maroons blast, waking the town.
Roar of boat leaving the harbour,
a large warmth gone from my bed.

Scott Thurston

A Bowl of Fruit

Und wars für diese schon zu viel, das Aufgehn?
  - Rilke, 'Die Rosenschale'

What comes of making something so
unnatural?

From the violence of an unpassed course –
a bowl of fruit.

Held heavy in blunt planes
a bunch of clustered objects in the mind.

A steady inwardness draws them in
pushes their clumsy order out

into the cosmos.

This junk
too far from space
is space itself.

Held together
it disintegrates.

Ars Moriendi

It is too late to research;
I just don't have time.

You will have to do that for me,
Afterwards. To check and see

Where I lie up with these tracts.
Historicize me. It seems that to

Confront my worst fear – of facing
A self-inflicted death – is what might

Lead to real living with others.
I am not dying yet we are all lying

Still.

Hard Bind

Collecting the new bound text
of uncertain shape; the possibilities

have multiplied beyond management.
At this point I am paused between

having to adopt a client's taste
and having a professional's eye.

But what is that eye and body
attached; stiffened into mimicry

of the material imperfections of objects?
Is this anything I can use

against the blank sheets the boards enclose?

Where is Love?

***

Where is love?
    Love has lost its way.
While in my heart its blind trueness
Sharpens like a needle every day.

If love is that name we give to
The best part of ourselves;
It's there when I choose to share
My dust with insects, their lives spare.

But not spare. Why should I be able
To choose? The quivering needle of an
Old compass points in the opposite direction –
It's been buried for too long.

Love has to be absolutely fought for:
To be cut out, lifted, poised
Aloft for a float in clear sky
    – it is the last word.

***

Where is thought?
    Thought has shot its last bold bolt
Twice in a heart-tree, its bland tiredness
Pulses like a minor motor way.

A blunt tab is that we pull over
Put upon the ruined counter
The worktop of choice with a charred
Coaster, a cracked lip, a screwdriver.

Buy not share my shoddy ware able to
Booze quivering guts in a holo-deck.
Starry points direct wrenched bridges
Burdened of hid samples.

Thought has to be absolutely feared absolutely
Cutting out on a free way chip board.
Trapped lights pull a float under
    – it's peeled off today.

★★★

It's lost that thought.
    It's shorn shod bold into a dry well,
Told twice to heat ray treatment for blind
Pulses in a ratchet mirror glance.

A heaving tub is what lights us
Pulled off a stripped sideboard.
The anvil of solace: a manky
Toaster, a bulging drawer, a flaming

My not share in dull life housing to
Snooze cruise a stunning blonde with
Several points northern direct trading co.
Busted triumphant.

That has to be it now tried to
Cut it out on the hold lamb supper
Of trawled bits negotiate the dive
    – the large day.

★★★

that it could be
a warning against itself
these small tensions
take their attention out
on me

if that's a measure
does it fake the
materiality – how to
find, ride the rind
of the welter

a skinless decision
rewound the bolus
a reflux smell
before the mouth
this public thinking

is terrifying
that it could be
an even patience
open my workshop
take me prisoner

★★★

Why does it need to be stated?
As if it were ever any less

than obvious. That time is past
now. It is still

here. Calls and conversation echo
in the street. I no longer want

to abstract these things that
impose their attention on me;

that I impose my attention on.
That was a way of avoiding

responsibility for them, for me, but also
a way of changing them.

The change still has to take place
at a different price. A diction cut

for a clean address: the swish discourse
nails a voice. But wobbles, cleanly

on it, off of it.

★★★

Book by cover lover lodged
lugged drawn into fallacies –

is yours a true one? Deep
rich or a shadowy shower

sunk wrapped wafer-thin around
a barking empty cask?

You stifle me the air full of men's
voices I can't wade through can't

even meet the mettle of
persuasion to cycle out lithe

platitudes cross lumps of ornate
fretwork a tight rope bridge

of tight hope.

Biographies / Acknowledgements

Avik Chanda's poems have appeared internationally, including *Other Poetry, Stride, Wolf, Richmond Review, Orbis, Fire* and *Octavo*. He divides his time between India, the UK and Europe. He publishes features, art reviews and short stories, and has exhibited his paintings solo. Acknowledgements to *Promise* (2003) for 'Nabami'; *Brittle Star* (2003) for 'Humayun's Tomb',; *Quarterly Literary Review Singapore* (2004) for 'Histories'; *Shearsman* (2004) for 'Torch Lamp Drawings'; and *Black Bear Review* (2002) for 'Malevich'.

Abi Curtis lives in Brighton and is studying for a DPhil in Creative and Critical Writing at the University of Sussex. She writes fiction and poetry and is completing a first collection. In 2004 she was awarded an Eric Gregory Award from the Society of Authors. Her poems are included in *Reactions 4, Five: A Book of Art, The South East Review, Popularity Contest, The London Review of Books* and the *Seren Selections* anthology in 2005.

Rose Flint is a poet, art therapist and creative writing tutor. She is currently the Lead Writer for the Kingfisher Project, working in the hospital and community of Salisbury. She has held two Poetry Places from the Poetry Society and a Year of the Artist Award. She tutors for both Ty Newydd and Arvon. Her three collections are *Blue Horse of Morning* (Seren), *Firesigns* (Poetry Salzburg) and *Nekyia* (Stride). Her work can be found in many magazines and anthologies including *The Rainbow's Quivering Tongue* (Stride).

Iain Galbraith's poems have been widely published in journals. He has translated many German and Austrian writers into English, and won the John Dryden Prize for Literary Translation in 2004 for his translations of Raoul Schrott's poetry. He also translates into German. Acknowledgements to the *TLS* for 'Skew' and 'Hacking into Forever', *PN Review* for 'The Voice', 'A Brim of Lather on the Bay of Cologne' and 'Passing the Steading', and satt.org for 'Wych Hazel'

Luke Kennard lives a life of hermetic solitude. His work – which many identify as an intellectual game deliberately obfuscating any true sense of identity – and his vituperative criticism – which many identify as a cry for help – has appeared in *Reactions, Stride* and *Orbis*. *The Solex Brothers* was recently published by Stride. He edits *Popularity Contest* and is a founder member of *Versus: The Campaign Against Poetry*. In 2005 he was awarded a Gregory Award from the Society of Authors.

Kit Lambert lives in Cardiff, where he came second in the Wales Award for Spoken Poetry 2003. His poems have appeared in Gavin Turk's edition of *Five* and *The Red Poets: Vol. 10* amongst others He is involved with Sgript Cymru, the national company for contemporary drama in Wales. His first full-length play, *The Custom House*, will be produced in Cardiff in 2005.

Sarah Law was born in Norwich and studied literature at Cambridge and London Universities. She has had work published in *Reactions, Pretext, Fire, The Paper, The Independent, Mudlark* and the *Tabla Book of New Verse*. Her poetry collections are *Bliss Tangle* (Stride, 1999) and *The Lady Chapel* (Stride, 2003). She is currently Academic Director for Creative Writing, Literature and Film Studies at Continuing Education, UEA. She regularly reviews poetry for *Orbis* and *Stride* magazines.

Aoife Mannix toured with the Renaissance One production *Kin* (2003/04) and Apples & Snakes *Writers on The Storm* (2002/03). She won the 2001 Farrago London Slam! and first prize in the Arts Angels Poetry Competition 2002. Her publications are *The Trick of Foreign Words* (Tall Lighthouse, 2002), *The Elephant In The Corner* (Tall Lighthouse, 2005) and the CD *Did You Forget To Take Your Tablets?* (with Richard Lewis). Her poems are widely anthologised and have been broadcast on BBC Radio 3, Radio 4 and the World Service.

Sophie Mayer published a first collection *Marsh Fear/Fen Tiger* as 'Sophie Levy' [with Leo Mellor] (Salt, 2002). In 2004 she was awarded an Eric Gregory award from the Society of Authors. She is currently completing a PhD on feminist literature and film at the University of Toronto, where she is poetry editor for *echolocation*. She toured with *Girls Who Bite Back: Witches, Mutants, Slayers, and Freaks*, a collection about feminism and contemporary pop culture (Sumach, 2004).

Joanne Merriam is a Canadian writer who lives in Tennessee with her husband and rabbit. Her first collection is *The Glaze from Breaking* (Stride, 2005). Acknowledgements to *The Fiddlehead* for 'Auto Biographies'; *Room of One's Own* for 'Guest Room'; *Pottersfield Portfolio* for 'Things that

Happened in My Absence'; *Quarry Magazine* for 'What Sharp Teeth You Have', and *Strange Horizons* for 'Mirror Points'. You can find her online at www.joannemerriam.com

George Messo is a poet, translator and editor. His first collection was *From the Pine Observatory* (Halfacrown Books, 2000) and *Entrances* is forthcoming from Shearsman. Recent work has appeared in *World Literature Today, Metamorphosis, Poetry Wales*, and *Translation Review*. He is a prolific translator from and into Turkish, with a first book in Turkish, *Aradaki Ses (The In-between Voice)* due in 2005. He divides his time between Ankara, Turkey, and Riyadh, Saudi Arabia, from where he edits the international literary journal *Near East Review.*

Anouk Mishti is of Sri Lankan origin and grew up in the U.S, Australia and England. She graduated from the University of Warwick, in English & Creative Writing, and works in the arts and cultural field. Much of her poetry is informed by her British sensibility and appreciation of humour, inspired by the lives and literature of women, particularly of South Asian origin. Acknowledgements to *Phoenix New Writing*, ed. David Morley (Heaventree Press, 2003) for 'I Look', 'No Pretence' and 'She Wore the Piano Keys'.

Jonathan Morley is a poet, teacher and community publisher. He holds an MA in Postcolonial Literature and teaches Creative and Academic Writing at Coventry University. He is co-Director of the Heaventree Press and the founder-editor of *Avocado* magazine. He is working on the forthcoming *Oxford Companion to Black British History* and undertaking a PhD at the University of Warwick on Modernism and Caribbean poetry.

Alan Mumford lives in north London. He has had poems published in *Reactions 4, Ambit, Poetry London, Poetry Wales* and *PEN International.*

Candy Neubert lived in Africa where she published her first book, *Zen Frog*. Her work has appeared recently in the *Rialto, London Magazine* and the *TLS*. She was runner-up in the Arvon and the National Poetry Competitions in 2000, and was a guest reader at the Aldeburgh Poetry Festival in 2002.

Linda Rose Parkes has an MA in Creative Writing from UEA. Her poems have been widely published, including *Reactions 4* (Pen&Inc). She worked in Germany with songwriters and musicians, before returning to her native Channel Island. Her first full collection is *The Usher's Torch* (Hearing Eye, 2005). Acknowledgements to *Leviathan* for 'Nanny's Coffee' and 'The Punter', and *Ambit* for 'In the Beginning was Menses' and 'The Curator'. 'The Distant Aunt' won second prize in the Keats-Shelley Memorial prize.

Jane Routh is a writer and photographer who also manages a flock of geese, some Ancient Semi-Natural Woodland and plants trees. Her collection *Circumnavigation* (Smith/Doorstop, 2002) was shortlisted for the Forward Prize Best First Collection and *Teach Yourself Mapmaking* (forthcoming Autumn 2006) is a Poetry Book Society recommendation. Acknowledgements to *Other Poetry* for 'MN 546 711' and 'The Red Cow'; *island* for 'Mealista'; *Stride* for 'On the Island' and 'Lineaments of and Afternoon', and *Poetry Review* for 'All My Dead' and 'Eleventh Hour'.

Sreejata Snyder was born in 1975 and grew up living in the residential compound of a powerhouse station near Calcutta, held by tall iron-railings and spirits from the Raj. She lived in Poona whilst studying for her BA and MA, and in Illinois whilst taking an MFA in Creative Writing. She now lives in Devon's Teign Valley and is writing poetry and criticism for a PhD at the University of Exeter.

Frances Thompson's poems have appeared widely in magazines and anthologies, including *Reactions*. Her first collection, *Feather in the Ground*, is forthcoming. She has been guest poet at several international conferences, including the 2004 Yeats Summer School in Sligo. She reviews for *The Journal*, and holds an MA in Creative Writing from the University of Exeter. Acknowledgements to *Worldspirit* for 'The Goat Bells'; *Nightingale* for 'Infintives', *Saw* for 'History Lesson' and to *Scintilla* for 'Mrs. Jones'.

Scott Thurston began writing in the late 1980s around Gilbert Adair's 'Subvoicive Poetry' reading series and Bob Cobbing's 'New River Project'. Publications include *Turns* (with Robert Sheppard) (Ship of Fools/Radiator, 2003), *Two Sequences* (RWC, 1998), *State(s)walk(s)* (Writers Forum, 1994) and *Poems Nov 89-Jun 91* (Writers Forum, 1991). He teaches English and Creative Writing at The University of Salford and runs the little magazine *The Radiator*.